TEXAS GUIDE TO LAWYER DISQUALIFICATION

2016

By

CHARLES HERRING, JR.
Partner
Herring & Panzer, L.L.P.

JASON M. PANZER
Partner
Herring & Panzer, L.L.P.

Horizon Legal Publishing

This book is not intended to offer advice or counsel. Nor is it intended to serve as a substitute for professional representation. Because the information in this book may not be sufficient to address a client's particular problem, and because this area of law constantly changes, lawyers and others using this publication should not rely on it as a substitute for independent research.

International Standard Book Number

978-0-9967858-1-5 (print)

978-0-9967858-0-8 (eBook)

About the Authors

Charles "Chuck" Herring, Jr. is a partner in the law firm of Herring & Panzer, L.L.P. Since 1985, he has been Board Certified in Civil Trial Law. For many years he has practiced primarily the law of lawyering—handling legal malpractice cases, and dealing with a vast array of legal ethics and professional responsibility issues, including advising lawyers, law firms, government entities, and clients. For over 25 years he has been the author of *Texas Legal Malpractice & Lawyer Discipline* (ALM rev. ed. 2015). He is coauthor with Professor Alex Albright of *Handbook of Texas Discovery Practice* (West Group rev. ed. 2015). The Texas Supreme Court has repeatedly appointed Chuck to its task forces and committees, including as Chair of the Statewide Task Force On Sanctions, and as a member of the Texas Supreme Court Advisory Committee, and a member of the Texas Supreme Court Grievance Oversight Committee. Chuck also has served on several State Bar of Texas committees, including as Chair of the Committee for the Prevention of Legal Malpractice. For many years, Chuck has taught at the Texas Center for Legal Ethics, instructing new lawyers on avoiding malpractice and grievance. Chuck also received the First Annual Professionalism Award from the Texas Center for Legal Ethics and the Travis County Bar Association. Before founding his current law firm, he was a litigation partner at Jones Day Reavis & Pogue. He is an Honors graduate of the University of Texas School of Law, and clerked for United States District Judge Owen D. Cox.

Jason Panzer is a partner in the law firm of Herring & Panzer, L.L.P. For over 15 years, he has focused his practice principally on the litigation of professional and legal malpractice lawsuits, and consulting with both lawyers and clients regarding the ethical duties and responsibilities of lawyers in Texas. In 2010, he was named Texas Super Lawyers Rising Star in the area of Professional Liability Plaintiff by Thomson Reuters, printed in Texas Monthly Magazine. Before joining Herring & Panzer, L.L.P., Mr. Panzer was with the law firm of Knisely, Prehoditch & Panzer, P.C.

Table of Contents

CHAPTER 1. INTRODUCTION

§ 1.1 Organization of This Volume 1

§ 1.2 Origins of Conflict of Interest Prohibitions 2

CHAPTER 2. PRACTICAL CONSIDERATIONS CONCERNING WHETHER TO SEEK OR OPPOSE DISQUALIFICATION

§ 2.1 Introduction 5

§ 2.2 Reasons to File a Motion to Disqualify 6

§ 2.3 Reasons Not to File a Motion to Disqualify 12

§ 2.4 Reasons to Oppose a Motion to Disqualify 15

§ 2.5 Reasons Not to Oppose a Motion to Disqualify 15

CHAPTER 3. THE ROLE OF DISCIPLINARY RULES IN DISQUALIFICATION PROCEEDINGS

§ 3.1 Introduction 17

§ 3.2 Technical Compliance or
     Violation Is Not Determinative 18

CHAPTER 4. FORMER-CLIENT CONFLICTS OF INTEREST: DISCIPLINARY RULE 1.09 AND THE SUBSTANTIAL-RELATIONSHIP STANDARD

§ 4.1 Introduction 20

§ 4.2 Disciplinary Rule 1.09: In General 20

§ 4.3 Disciplinary Rule 1.09(a)(3): The Same or
     Substantially Related Matter 21

§ 4.4 Disciplinary Rule 1.09(a)(2): Violation
     of Confidentiality 26

§ 4.5 Disciplinary Rule 1.09(a)(1): Questioning
     Lawyer's Services or Work Product 28

§ 4.6 Rule 1.09(b)-(c): Imputation of Conflicts of Interest   28

§ 4.7 Rule 1.09(a): Personal Attorney-Client Relationship   31

§ 4.8 Disqualification Exception: Client Consent   31

CHAPTER 5. DISCIPLINARY RULE 1.06 — CONCURRENT CONFLICT OF INTERESTS

§ 5.1 Introduction   33

§ 5.2 Rule 1.06(a): the prohibition against representing opposing parties in the same matter   34

§ 5.3 Rule 1.06(b): the substantially-related-matter and reasonable appearance prohibitions   35

§ 5.4 Rule 1.06(c): consent; consentable and nonconsentable conflicts   36

§ 5.5 Rule 1.06(d): conflicts arising from prior representation of multiple clients in a matter   40

§ 5.6 Withdrawal from representation   41

§ 5.7 Imputation of Rule 1.06 conflicts   42

CHAPTER 6. DISCIPLINARY RULE 1.10 — SUCCESSIVE GOVERNMENT AND PRIVATE EMPLOYMENT

§ 6.1 Introduction   43

§ 6.2 A former government lawyer who represents a private client   44

§ 6.3 A former government lawyer who has confidential government information   45

§ 6.4 A lawyer who moves from private practice to government employment   46

§ 6.5 A government lawyer who negotiates for private employment   47

§ 6.6 A lawyer who moves from one government agency to another   47

CHAPTER 7. DISCIPLINARY RULE 1.11 — ADJUDICATORY OFFICIAL OR LAW CLERK

§ 7.1 Introduction — 48

§ 7.2 A former judge or law clerk in private practice — 48

§ 7.3 A judge or law clerk negotiating for employment — 52

CHAPTER 8. DISCIPLINARY RULE 3.08 — LAWYER AS WITNESS

§ 8.1 Introduction — 53

§ 8.2 Rule 3.08 as a disqualification standard — 54

§ 8.3 Policy considerations for the lawyer-as-witness prohibition — 56

§ 8.4 Testimony on behalf of a client — Rule 3.08(a) — 58

§ 8.5 Testimony adverse to a client — Rule 3.08(b) — 60

§ 8.6 Participation of other lawyers in a disqualified lawyer's firm — Rule 3.08(c) — 61

§ 8.7 Participation of a disqualified lawyer-witness in a role other than in-court advocate — Rule 3.08(c) — 62

CHAPTER 9. JOINT DEFENSE AGREEMENTS

§ 9.1 Introduction — 63

§ 9.2 Disqualification standard — 63

CHAPTER 10. DISQUALIFICATION OF COCOUNSEL

§ 10.1 Introduction — 66

§ 10.2 The *American Home* standards — 66

CHAPTER 11. DISQUALIFICATION OF SUCCESSOR COUNSEL

§ 11.1 Introduction — 71

§ 11.2 *In re George* standards — 71

CHAPTER 12. DISQUALIFICATION FOR RECEIPT OF PRIVILEGED INFORMATION

§ 12.1 Introduction 74

§ 12.2 *In re Meador* 74

§ 12.3 *In re Nitla* 79

§ 12.4 *In re RSR Corp.* 80

CHAPTER 13. DISQUALIFICATIONS RESULTING FROM NONLAWYER STAFF

§ 13.1 Introduction 82

§ 13.2 Nonlawyer staff disqualifications: in general 82

§ 13.3 Nonlawyer disqualification decisions:
Texas Supreme Court 84

§ 13.4 Nonlawyer disqualification decisions:
Court of Appeals 89

CHAPTER 14. DISCIPLINARY RULE 4.02 — THE ANTI-CONTACT RULE

§ 14.1 Introduction 92

§ 14.2 Communications with represented persons 93

§ 14.3 Communication with retained experts 95

§ 14.4 Employees of opposing entity-party 96

§ 14.5 Second opinions 97

§ 14.6 Other remedies for Rule 4.02 violations 98

CHAPTER 15. OTHER GROUNDS FOR DISQUALIFICATION

§ 15.1 Introduction 99

§ 15.2 Other disciplinary rules 99

§ 15.3 Other disciplinary rules: Rule 1.15 99

§ 15.4 Other disciplinary rules: Rule 7.06 101

§ 15.5 Other rules 104

§ 15.6 Statutes and regulations 104

§ 15.7 Disqualification as an inherent-power sanction 105

CHAPTER 16. IMPUTATION AND SCREENING

§ 16.1 Imputation and screening: in general   108

§ 16.2 Imputation under Rules 1.06, 1.07, and 1.08   109

§ 16.3 Imputation under Rule 1.09   110

§ 16.4 Screening: in general   112

§ 16.5 Screening of nonlawyers   113

§ 16.6 Screening: determining whether screening
     is effective   115

§ 16.7 Screening under Rules 1.10 and 1.11   119

CHAPTER 17. WAIVER OF DISQUALIFICATION

§ 17.1 Waiver by delay   120

§ 17.2 Other waivers   121

§ 17.3 Explaining delay   122

CHAPTER 18. DISQUALIFICATION IN FEDERAL COURT

§ 18.1 Introduction   123

§ 18.2 Federal court decisions   125

CHAPTER 19. PRACTICAL TIPS FOR DISQUALIFICATION

§ 19.1 Introduction   129

§ 19.2 Steps to take in seeking disqualification   129

§ 19.3 Steps to take in opposing disqualification   135

CHAPTER 20. LIST OF PRINCIPAL TEXAS DECISIONS ADDRESSING LAWYER DISQUALIFICAITON

138

CHAPTER 21. LIST OF PEC OPINIONS ADDRESSING PRINCIPAL CONFLICT OF INTEREST RULES

163

SHORTENED CITE FORMS

For convenience in this volume, the following shortened citation forms are used:

"Texas Rules" or "Rules," for the Texas Disciplinary Rules of Professional Conduct

"Model Rules," for the American Bar Association's Model Rules of Professional Conduct

"Restatement," for the Restatement (Third) of the Law Governing Lawyers

Chapter 1

Introduction

§ 1.1 Organization of this volume. This volume is organized as follows:

- Chapter 1 explains the organization of this volume, and the origins of conflict of interest prohibitions that provide the foundation for many types of motions to disqualify counsel.

- Chapter 2 discusses practical considerations for lawyers and parties to consider in determining whether to file or oppose a motion to disqualify.

- Chapter 3 discusses the role of the disciplinary rules in disqualification proceedings.

- Chapters 4 through 15 discuss various grounds for disqualification.

- Chapter 16 discusses imputation of conflicts and the effect of screening in various settings.

- Chapter 17 addresses waiver doctrines that apply to disqualification.

- Chapter 18 addresses disqualification standards in federal court.

- Chapter 19 sets out practical tips for pursuing or opposing motions to disqualify.

- Chapter 20 lists most of the state and federal decisions in Texas concerning disqualification, and the issues that those decisions address.

§ 1.2 Origins of conflict of interest prohibitions. Most disqualifications of counsel result from conflicts of interest.[1] Legal prohibitions against conflicts of interest are ancient in origin. For example, some court decisions still cite the conflict-of-interest condemnation expressed in the Bible, Matthew 6:24:

> No man can serve two masters: for either he will hate the one, and love the other; or else he will hold to the one, and despise the other. Ye cannot serve God and mammon.[2]

Statutory predecessors of modern conflict-of-interest prohibitions have also existed for several centuries.[3] But even earlier, Roman civil law recognized fiduciary duties that led to some of the modern legal ethics rules concerning conflict of interest. Indeed, the Latin origin of the term is *fiduciarius*—meaning "holding in trust." Roman Praetors, who acted as magistrates, applied certain fiduciary concepts and protections in relationships involving special trust, including between parents and children, patrons and freedmen, and guardians and wards.[4]

---

[1] See Chapter 15, concerning other grounds for disqualification.

[2] *See, e.g., In re Texas Windstorm Insurance Ass'n*, 417 S.W.3d 119, 133 (Tex. App.—Houston [1st Dist.] 2013, orig. proceeding) (quoting Matthew 6:24); *J.K. & Susie L. Wadley Research Institute & Blood Bank v. Morris*, 776 S.W.2d 271, 284 (Tex. App.—Dallas 1989, orig. proceeding) (Howell, J., concurring).

[3] *See* City of London Ordinance of 1280 A.D. ("He who takes from both parties and is attainted thereof shall be suspended for three years; where one takes [money] and then leaves his client and leagues himself with the other party and where one takes [money] and abandons his client let such person return twofold and not be heard against the client in that plea." (quoted in Herman Cohen, *A History of The English Bar and Attornatus To 1450,* p.234 (1929)).

[4] *See, e.g.,* Lester Brickman, *Attorney-Client Fee Arbitration: A Dissenting View*, 1990 Utah L. Rev. 277, 282-83 n. 38 (1990) ("The origin of fiduciary obligation can be traced to Roman Civil law. . . . Doctrines of fiduciary law arose out of matters entrusted to the Roman Praetors. Praetors

Thus, in many formulations in many different contexts, the law has developed key fiduciary concepts applicable when one person in a relationship of trust has special knowledge or power or control over another. Such duties typically include loyalty (including the duty to avoid impermissible conflicts of interest), honesty, full disclosure, and protection of property and confidential information.[5]

Modern legal ethics codes and rules have codified and refined these concepts. In 1908, the American Bar Association adopted the Canons of Ethics. Several of the canons reflected the preexisting fiduciary duties. For example, Canon 6 stated, in part, that "[i]t is unprofessional to represent conflicting interests, except by express consent of all concerned given after a full disclosure of the facts."[6] More recent versions of national and state codes and rules of legal ethics have further refined and articulated those preexisting fiduciary duties. In 1969, the ABA replaced the Canons of Ethics with the Code of Professional Responsibility, and in 1983 the Model Rules of Professional Responsibility replaced the Code.[7]

---

were municipal officers of the city of Rome and acted as chief judicial magistrates. . . . Matters reserved to the Praetor's adjudication included . . . claims to trusts under wills; pleas for support, child from parent, freedman from patron; questions arising between master and slave; fees and honoraria for certain professional classes, such as judicial assessors and those who managed the affairs of others; and the removal of guardians who proved unsuitable in the oversight of their wards.").

[5] *See, e.g., Willis v. Maverick,* 760 S.W.2d 642, 645 (Tex. 1988) ("A fiduciary relationship exists between an attorney and client. As a fiduciary, an attorney is obligated to render a full and fair disclosure of facts material to the client's representation.") (citations omitted); Comm. On Pattern Jury Charges, State Bar Of Texas, Texas Pattern Jury Charges: Business, Consumer, Insurance & Employment PJC 104.2 (2014); Restatement (Third) of the Law Governing Lawyers § 16(3) & cmts. b, e, § 49 cmt. b.

[6] *See also* Canon 11 (concerning protection of client property); Canon 37 (concerning protection of a client's confidential information).

[7] The corresponding Texas changes were the adoption of the Texas Code of Professional Responsibility in 1971, and the Texas Disciplinary Rules of

As one federal court decision expressed the continuing interaction between the underlying fiduciary duties and legal ethics rules, the rules "significantly inform the analysis of the scope of fiduciary duties between attorneys and their clients, as well as between attorneys and their former clients."[1]

Professional Conduct in 1990.

[1] *Sealed Party v. Sealed Party*, 2006 WL 1207732, at *8 (S.D. Tex. 2006).

Chapter 2

Practical Considerations Concerning
Whether To Seek or Oppose Disqualification

"I will not seek . . . disqualification unless it is necessary for protection of my client's lawful objectives or is fully justified by the circumstances." Texas Lawyer's Creed, Article III(19)

"For to win one hundred victories in one hundred battles is not the acme of skill. To subdue the enemy without fighting is the acme of skill." Sun-tzu, *The Art of War*

§ 2.1 Introduction.

Often the best thing to do with a strong motion to disqualify counsel is to not file it—or even mention it. Why? Because disqualifying one opposing counsel usually just results in new counsel. A party may spend substantial time and money to disqualify one lawyer, only to face another lawyer, and perhaps an even better lawyer. On the other hand, filing a motion to disqualify—even a weak motion—is sometimes exactly the right tactic. Most importantly, in some cases prevailing on the motion is necessary to protect a client's confidential information. But before filing a motion to disqualify, carefully consider the pros and cons.

Similarly, if a lawyer or firm becomes a target of a motion to disqualify, the first question to ask is whether to oppose the motion. The answer requires pragmatic, detached analysis. A common initial reaction is anger. That's normal. After all, the motion has attacked or called into question counsel's ethics and professional standards. But opposing a meritorious motion to disqualify can waste a client's time and money—for which the target lawyer ultimately may be liable. Being disqualified can have several unpleasant collateral consequences for a lawyer or firm, including the disqualification, loss of potential future fees, disgorgement of past fees, time and expense in opposing the motion, loss of the client (or, sometimes, two sets of clients), disciplinary consequences, and a suit for malpractice or breach of fiduciary duty.

§ 2.2 Reasons To File A Motion To Disqualify.

1. To Protect The Client's Confidential Information. Protecting a client's confidential information is usually the best reason to file a motion to disqualify counsel. Most disqualification motions address former-client conflicts of interest. Former-client conflicts frequently arise when a lawyer first represents a client in one matter, and then later represents a party adverse to the former client. Rule 1.09 is the principal former-client-conflict rule, and two of the three prohibitions in the Rule address protection of confidential client information. Rule 1.09(a)(2) prohibits a lawyer from being adverse to a former client if the new representation "in reasonable probability will involve a violation of the Rule 1.05 [the confidential-information rule]." Rule 1.09(a)(3) prohibits representation adverse to a former client in "the same or a substantially related matter." Comment 4B explains the central rationale of the substantially-related prohibition: "it primarily involves situations where a lawyer could have acquired confidential information concerning a prior client that could be used either to that prior client's disadvantage or for the advantage of the lawyer's current client or some other person." Thus, protection of a client's confidential information is a key rationale.

Rule 4.02, the anti-contact rule, also seeks to prevent

"efforts to circumvent the lawyer-client relationship existing between other persons . . . and their respective counsel."[1]

In some cases, having adverse counsel in a position to use a former client's confidential information against the former client could seriously prejudice the former client. That prospect well may justify filing the motion to disqualify. If opposing counsel had a former-client relationship and now possesses the former client's confidential information that could be useful in the present litigation, that can be a very compelling reason to seek disqualification.

2. To Disqualify Counsel Who May Appear More Credible Because of the Former-Client Relationship. The third restriction in Rule 1.09(a) prohibits representation adverse to the former client when the lawyer "questions the validity of the lawyer's services or work product for the former client."[2] The classic example is the lawyer who drafts a will and then represents an heir seeking to set aside or avoid some provision of the will. That type of situation is both extreme and rare. But when it does occur, the lawyer who is purportedly explaining, interpreting, or arguing the meaning of his or his firm's work product can have enhanced credibility before the jury: "I [or my firm] wrote this document. We are in the best position to know what it means." That is a serious problem for the former client.

A similar consideration underlies the lawyer-as-witness rule, Rule 3.08. As Comment 4 to the Rule recognizes, a lawyer who acts as both advocate and witness in a matter can confuse a factfinder, especially a jury.

---

[1] Rule 4.02 cmt. 1.

[2] Rule 1.09(a)(1).

3. <u>To Vindicate The Duty of Loyalty</u>. Comment 1 to Rule 1.06 states a core principle of the attorney-client relationship: "Loyalty is an essential element in the lawyer's relationship to a client." Loyalty includes avoiding improper conflicts of interest. Apart from the Disciplinary Rules, loyalty is a fiduciary duty at the heart of the attorney-client relationship.[3] Understandably, a lawyer's disloyalty in the form of conflicts of interest can upset and anger clients, former clients, juries, and judges. Vindicating that interest is entirely proper.

4. <u>To Deter Future Violations and Avoid Waiver</u>. When a lawyer's representation of a corporate client terminates, and then the lawyer improperly accepts representation adverse to the former client, the former client may want to pursue disqualification to deter future, similar violations, and to avoid waiver arguments. That's true even if the current case is small and unimportant. Consider an in-house counsel who represents a corporate client in groundwater contamination matters and then leaves the corporate employment for private practice and accepts representation in a groundwater-contamination case against the former corporate employer-client. Even if the first case adverse to the former employer is financially insignificant, the former client-employer may want to pursue disqualification in order to deter future, adverse representation. Diligently protecting the client's confidential information and attacking the former counsel's disloyalty also may send a useful, deterrent message to other current lawyer-

---

[3] *See, e.g.*, Comm. on Pattern Jury Charges, State Bar of Texas, Texas Pattern Jury Charges: Business, Consumer, Insurance, Employment, PJC 104.2 (Questions and Instruction—Breach of Fiduciary Duty; providing that a fiduciary must show that the fiduciary "placed the interests of [the client] before his own . . . and did not place himself in any position where his self-interest might conflict with his obligation as a fiduciary . . . .").

employees who might be tempted to leave employment and engage in similar adverse representation.

5. <u>To Achieve Tactical Advantages</u>. Texas case law and the Disciplinary Rules generally discourage the use of motions to disqualify to achieve "tactical" advantage. For example, the Texas Supreme Court has repeatedly stated that courts "must adhere to an exacting standard" when considering motions to disqualify in order "to discourage their use as a dilatory trial tactic."[4] In disqualification proceedings under Rule 3.08, when a lawyer proposes to act as both advocate and witness, Comment 10 to that Rule expressly cautions against using a disqualification motion as a "tactical weapon" to deprive the opposing party of chosen counsel.

Nonetheless, lawyers and their clients often seek "tactical" advantages in litigation. Some tactics are legitimate, others aren't.[5] Among the possible and potentially advantageous and legitimate tactical benefits to consider, depending on the particular facts, are the following:

    a. <u>Delay</u>. Filing an invalid motion to disqualify solely to delay a trial is both improper and sanctionable.[6] But a meritorious motion, whether

---

[4] *See Spears v. Fourth Court of Appeals*, 797 S.W.2d 654, 656 (Tex. 1990, orig. proceeding); *NCNB Texas Nat'l Bank v. Coker*, 765 S.W.2d 398, 399 (Tex. 1989, orig. proceeding).

[5] In the broadest sense, almost every motion is a "tactic." *See, e.g., Black's Law Dictionary* 1681 (Bryan A. Garner ed., 10th ed., Thompson Reuters 2014) (defining "tactic" as including: "1. An adroit or artful maneuver, esp. against an adversary. 2. A method of employing or redirecting force in combat."); *cf.* Rule 1.02 cmt. 1 ("[A] lawyer has very broad discretion to determine technical and legal tactics, subject to the client's wishes regarding such matters as the expense to be incurred and concern for third persons who might be adversely affected.").

[6] *See, e.g.*, Tex. Civ. Prac. & Rem. Code § 10.001(1) (providing that by signing a motion, a lawyer certifies that the motion is not being presented

or not successful, almost inevitably causes delay. Indeed, motions to disqualify can require weeks or months to litigate to conclusion. The proceedings can generate substantial discovery, entail days or weeks of hearings, and produce emergency appeals and mandamus review. If a party's counsel is disqualified, the party must retain new counsel, who then must "catch up" with what has happened in the case. Catching up involves obtaining the former lawyers' file, documents, and other information, analyzing the file, meeting and talking with the client and client's representatives, etc.

In some cases even the process of obtaining prior counsel's file can be a challenging, time-consuming process. If prior, disqualified counsel improperly possessed a former client's confidential information, *In re George*[7] requires that counsel and the court follow proper file-transfer procedures to avoid tainting new counsel.

Delay may be both unavoidable and substantial—and it may be in the movant-client's interest.

b. <u>Expense</u>. Filing a motion to disqualify solely to increase litigation costs for the opposing party is both improper and sanctionable.[8]

---

for "any improper purpose, including . . . to cause unnecessary delay"); Rule 3.02 ("In the course of litigation, a lawyer shall not take a position that . . . unreasonably delays resolution of the matter.").

[7] 28 S.W.3d 511 (Tex. 2000). See Chapter 11, below.

[8] *See, e.g.*, Tex. Civ. Prac. & Rem. Code § 10.001(1) (providing that by signing a motion, a lawyer certifies that the motion is not being presented for "any improper purpose, including . . . to cause . . . needless increase in the cost of litigation"); Rule 3.02 ("In the course of litigation, a lawyer

But sometimes, litigating a valid motion to disqualify can be unavoidably expensive. The proceedings may require depositions, expert testimony, evidentiary hearings, extensive legal briefing, motions to stay, and mandamus review or direct appeal. In large cases, parties can spend hundreds of thousands of dollars, or more, litigating disqualification. When the movant has vast resources and the opposing party is underfinanced, the tactical advantage is obvious. Filing a motion solely to exploit that disparity would be improper. But the fact that such a disparity exists does not per se make pursuing a motion improper.

c. <u>Malpractice, grievance predicate</u>. A lawyer who undertakes improperly conflicted representation against a current or former client may end up facing a lawsuit, a grievance, or both. The conflict of interest may create liability to a former client who has to pay current counsel to pursue disqualification and who may incur other damages. If the trial court grants a motion to disqualify and expressly finds a violation of Rule 1.06 or 1.09, then the disqualified lawyer may be subject to a disciplinary complaint for the rule violation. Disciplinary authorities tend to give considerable weight to a judicial disciplinary referral or an express judicial finding of a rule violation. Thus, a former client may want to pursue disqualification, in part, to explore the viability of those additional remedies or to lay a predicate for those claims.

---

shall not take a position that unreasonably increases the costs . . . of the case . . . .").

d. Disqualifying particular opposing counsel. Sometimes a party reasonably believes that a particular opposing counsel has special skill or influence, perhaps with the presiding judge or a local jury, or special ability in a particular type of litigation. A valid disqualification motion that results in new, less "dangerous" opposing counsel may have important tactical benefits.

e. Basis for sanctions. A trial court that disqualifies a lawyer also may impose monetary or other sanctions against the lawyer. For example, the court may conclude that the lawyer who has engaged in disqualifying conduct also has engaged in discovery abuse or other sanctionable misconduct.

f. Eliminate opposing counsel. In some cases, if the party moving for disqualification succeeds, the opposing party will be unable to afford new counsel and will have to continue pro se.

The general principle is that pursuing a motion to disqualify counsel solely in order to obtain any of these possible tactical advantages can be improper. But for a lawyer and client to be aware of the likely benefits of pursuing a valid, successful motion to disqualify is reasonable and prudent.[9]

§ 2.3 Reasons Not To File A Motion To Disqualify.

1. To Avoid Replacing One Lawyer With Another and Incurring Additional Expense. When a court disqualifies counsel, usually another lawyer enters

---

[9] *Cf.* Rule 1.03(b) ("A lawyer shall explain a matter to the extent reasonably necessary to permit the client to make informed decisions regarding the representation.").

the case. In important litigation involving well-funded parties, disqualifying an excellent law firm just brings in another excellent law firm. Why waste the time and money? Worse, the lawyer who replaces the first lawyer may be a more experienced and skilled opponent.

2. To Avoid Litigating Insignificant Violations. Sometimes a lawyer improperly undertakes representation adverse to a former client, but the confidential information that the lawyer possesses is insignificant and could not prejudice the former client. For example, the former-client-conflict prohibition in Rule 1.09(a)(2) generally focuses on whether "in reasonable probability the representation will involve a violation of Rule 1.05 [the confidential-information rule]." But not all confidentiality violations are damaging. The confidentiality rule is quite broad. It encompasses both information protected by the attorney-client privilege and all other information "relating to a client or furnished by the client" that the lawyer acquires during or by reason of the representation.[10] A common setting involves a law firm associate who moves from one firm to another; at the first firm the associate worked on a minor, single-issue memo for a client; at the new firm, the associate has no significant involvement in the case adverse to the former client. In that situation, why bother to attempt to disqualify the associate's new law firm? Unless other, legitimate reasons exist—including those discussed in § 2.2, above—disqualification may not be warranted.

---

[10] Rule 1.05(a).

3. <u>To Avoid Unnecessarily Alienating Opposing Counsel</u>. Motions to disqualify often are inflammatory. They tend to anger and alienate the targeted opposing counsel. The motion usually alleges disciplinary-rule and ethical violations. No lawyer wants to confront those allegations, much less the possible collateral consequences of a disciplinary action or a liability claim. If the motion fails, hard feelings may poison the relationship between counsel throughout the entire litigation. Most lawyers want to avoid developing a reputation for Rambo-litigation tactics by filing unnecessary disqualification motions. As Article III.19 of the Texas Lawyer's Creed states, a lawyer should not seek disqualification unless it is "necessary for protection of [the] client's lawful objectives or is fully justified by the circumstances."

4. <u>To Avoid Offending The Judge</u>. Judges tend to dislike motions to disqualify. Hearings can be unpleasant, full of heated rhetoric and intense emotions. If a judge has to disqualify counsel, the disqualified lawyer or firm may resent the judge's decision, even if correct. The judge may have an ethical obligation to refer the lawyer to disciplinary authorities.[11] A lawyer should think carefully before putting a judge in that position.

5. <u>Other Remedies May Be Available</u>. If a disqualifying conflict does not pose a risk of significant damage, it may be feasible to negotiate a

---

[11] *See* Texas Code of Judicial Conduct, Canon 3D(2) (requiring a judge to make a disciplinary referral when the judge knows that a lawyer has committed a Disciplinary Rule violation that raises "a substantial question" concerning the lawyer's honesty, trustworthiness, or fitness).

contractual screening agreement.[12] The agreement can provide that the lawyer will not disclose any information concerning the former client to anyone in the new firm and will not work on the case or receive any information about the case. In some cases, that type of agreement provides sufficient practical protection and also avoids the substantial expense and other potential negative effects of litigating a motion to disqualify.

§ 2.4 Reasons To Oppose A Motion To Disqualify.

1. To Defeat An Invalid Motion And Avoid Unnecessary Adverse Consequences. A motion to disqualify can be expensive for both the targeted counsel and that counsel's client. The motion can lead to liability claims and disciplinary complaints against the targeted counsel. The client may incur the delay and expense of finding new counsel.

2. To Avoid Setting An Unfavorable Precedent. A lawyer who is the target of a motion to disqualify in a setting that may occur repeatedly in the future has an interest in not setting an unfavorable precedent by agreeing to disqualification or by losing a disqualification hearing. If the lawyer's current client also may face similar, repetitious litigation, the client may have the same interest to protect the right to retain the lawyer.

§ 2.5 Reasons Not To Oppose A Motion To Disqualify.

1. To Avoid Contesting A Valid Motion. Some motions to disqualify are valid. If a current or

---

[12] Absent that type of agreement, screening of lawyers is generally ineffective to avoid disqualification. *See* Chapter 16.

former client or even a litigation opponent raises a potentially legitimate challenge, the targeted lawyer and firm should carefully consider the potential consequences of contesting the matter. Fighting the matter will take time and money. If the lawyer's mistake caused the problem (e.g., an inadequate conflicts search during client intake), the lawyer likely will bear the expense, without reimbursement from the client. Even worse, in addition to the time and expense of fighting the matter, both the current and former client may be able to assert a liability claim and file grievances.

2. To Avoid Expense and Delay. Even an invalid disqualification motion may generate expense and delay. In some cases, targeted counsel may conclude that staying in the case is not worth the cost and delay to the client and counsel.

Chapter 3

The Role of Disciplinary Rules
In Disqualification Proceedings

§ 3.1 Introduction.

The Texas Supreme Court has repeatedly emphasized that Texas courts should refer to the Disciplinary Rules for "guidance" in deciding motions to disqualify counsel.[1] The "guidelines" are not controlling standards,[2] but as a practical matter a clear violation of a conflict-of-interest rule usually results in

---

[1] *Henderson v. Floyd*, 891 S.W.2d 252, 253 (Tex. 1995); *accord In re Cerberus Capital Management, L.P.*, 164 S.W.3d 379, 382 (Tex. 2005) ("The Disciplinary Rules, although promulgated as disciplinary standards rather than rules of procedural disqualification, provide guidelines relevant to a disqualification determination."); *In re Nitla S.A de C.V.*, 92 S.W.3d 419, 422 (Tex. 2002) ("[t]his [c]ourt often looks to the disciplinary rules to decide disqualification issues [.]"); *In re Users Sys. Servs., Inc.*, 22 S.W.3d 331, 334 (Tex. 1999); *In re EPIC Holdings, Inc.*, 985 S.W.2d 41, 48 (Tex. 1998); *Anderson Producing v. Koch Oil Co.*, 929 S.W.2d 416, 421 (Tex. 1996) ("We have recognized that 'the rule articulates considerations relevant to a procedural disqualification determination.' *Ayres v. Canales*, 790 S.W.2d 554, 556 n. 2 (Tex. 1990). We applied rule 3.08 as the standard for disqualification in *Ayres*, noting as follows: 'Indeed, it would be injudicious for this court to employ a rule of disqualification that could not be reconciled with the Texas Rules of Professional Conduct. Accordingly, we will refer to the rule for guidance in determining whether the trial court abused its discretion in [granting the motion to disqualify].'").

[2] *See, e.g., In re de Brittingham*, 319 S.W.3d 95, 98 (Tex. App.—San Antonio 2010, orig. proceeding) ("We look to the disciplinary rules to decide disqualification issues, but the disciplinary rules are merely guidelines and not controlling standards for motions to disqualify."); *Smith v. Abbott*, 311 S.W.3d 62, 73 (Tex. App.—Austin 2010, pet. denied) (the rules "are not binding" but courts look to them as "guidelines in determining whether attorney conduct warrants disqualification."); *City of Dallas v. Redbird Dev. Corp.*, 143 S.W.3d 375, 387 (Tex. App.—Dallas 2004, no pet.) ("A court often looks to the disciplinary rules to decide disqualification issues . . . . However, the disciplinary rules are merely guidelines—not controlling standards—for disqualification motions . . . .").

disqualification. However, disqualification is possible even in the absence of a rule violation.[3]

§ 3.2 Technical Compliance Or Violation Is Not Determinative.

Technical compliance with the Rules will not necessarily determine the outcome of a motion to disqualify. Nor will a technical violation. As the Texas Supreme Court stated in *In re Users Sys. Servs., Inc.*, "[t]echnical compliance with ethical rules might not foreclose disqualification, and by the same token, a violation of ethical rules might not require disqualification."[4]

Disqualification may be appropriate even without a rule violation. The Texas Supreme Court stated in *In re Meador*[5] that "[b]ased on our repeated statements that the disciplinary rules are only guidelines for disqualification motions, and the holding in [*National Medical Enters. v. Godbey*, 924 S.W. 2d 123 (Tex. 1996)], it is clear that a court has the power, under appropriate circumstances, to disqualify an attorney even though he or she has not violated a specific disciplinary rule."[6] In *Meador* the court set out standards for disqualifying counsel who improperly receive privileged information.[7] In *Godbey* the court required disqualification based on a joint-defense

---

[3] *In re User Sys. Servs., Inc.*, 22 S.W.3d 331 (Tex. 1991); *see also In re Meador*, 968 S.W.2d 346, 350 (Tex. 1998) ("We have often looked to our disciplinary rules to decide disqualification issues . . . . We have emphasized, however, that the disciplinary rules are merely guidelines— not necessarily controlling standards—for such motions.").

[4] 22 S.W.3d 331, 334 (Tex. 1991).

[5] 968 S.W.2d 346, 350 (Tex. 1998).

[6] *Accord In re NITLA S.A. de C.V.*, 92 S.W.3d 419, 422 (Tex. 2002) ("[Under appropriate circumstances, a trial court has the power to disqualify a lawyer even if he has not violated a specific disciplinary rule.")

[7] *See* Chapter 12.

agreement.[8] Neither case involved a specific disciplinary rule violation.

---

[8] *See* Chapter 9.

Chapter 4

Former-Client Conflicts of Interest:
Disciplinary Rule 1.09 And
The Substantial-Relationship Standard

§ 4.1 Introduction.

The most common ground for motions to disqualify counsel is a former-client conflict of interest, based on the substantial-relationship test. That standard now appears in Rule 1.09(a) (3), but existed in common law before Texas adopted the current Rules in 1990. However, as discussed below, Rule 1.09 provides two other grounds for disqualification.

§ 4.2 Disciplinary Rule 1.09: In General.

Rule 1.09 is the former-client conflicts rule. Rule 1.09(a) states three prohibitions:

> Without prior consent, a lawyer who personally has formerly represented a client in a matter shall not thereafter represent another person in a matter adverse to the former client:
>
>> (1) in which such other person questions the validity of the lawyer's services or work product for the former client;
>>
>> (2) if the representation in reasonable probability will involve a violation of Rule 1.05 [the confidentiality rule]; or
>>
>> (3) if it is the same or a substantially related matter.

Texas appellate court decisions have relied on each of those prohibitions for "guidance"[1] in determining motions to disqualify.

§ 4.3 Disciplinary Rule 1.09(a)(3): The Same Or Substantially Related Matter.

Rule 1.09(a)(3) generally prohibits a lawyer from representing a client in a matter adverse to a former client if the matter is "the same" or "a substantially related" matter.

For a lawyer to switch sides in the "same" matter is both unusual and egregious. The prohibition applies even if the lawyer withdrew from the prior representation "before the client [discloses] any confidential information."[2]

However, motions to disqualify under Rule 1.09(a)(3) usually focus on the other prohibition: whether the current representation is "substantially related" to the matter in which the lawyer previously represented the former client. This is the so-called substantial-relationship test for disqualification. Texas case law recognized this basis for disqualification well before adoption of the Texas Disciplinary Rules of Professional Conduct.[3]

---

[1] See Chapter 3, above.

[2] Rule 1.09 cmt. 4A.

[3] Effective January 1, 1990, the Texas Disciplinary Rules of Professional Conduct replaced the previous Texas Code of Professional Responsibility. By then, the substantial-relationship standard was well-established in Texas and many other states. *See, e.g., P & M Electric Co. v. Godard*, 478 S.W.2d 79, 80-81 (Tex. 1972) (approving and adopting the substantial-relationship test, as formulated in *T. C. Theatre Corp. v. Warner Bros. Pictures*, 113 F. Supp. 265 (S.D.N.Y. 1953)); *NCNB Tex. Nat'l Bank v. Coker*, 765 S.W.2d 398, 399-400 (Tex. 1989) ("When contemplating whether disqualification of counsel is proper, the court must determine whether the matters embraced within the pending suit are *substantially related* to the factual matters involved in the previous suit."; and further stating that the movant must show "facts indicating a substantial relation between the two representations. The moving party must prove the existence of a prior

The substantially-related prohibition in Rule 1.09(a)(3) "primarily" involves situations in which a lawyer "could have acquired confidential information concerning a prior client that could be used either to that prior client's disadvantage or for the advantage of the lawyer's current client or some other person."[4] To that extent, the prohibition overlaps with the prohibition in Rule 1.09(a)(2) against representation when a reasonable probability exists that the new representation will violate the confidentiality rule (Rule 1.05). However, another rationale for the substantial-relationship standard is the duty of loyalty that is an "essential element" in a lawyer's relationship with a client.[5]

In *Texaco, Inc. v. Garcia*, for example, the Texas Supreme Court stated that the substantial-relationship standard requires the movant to establish two elements:

[1.] the existence of a prior attorney-client relationship,

[2.] in which the factual matters involved were so related to the facts in the pending litigation that it creates a genuine threat that confidences revealed to his former counsel will be divulged to his present adversary.[6]

---

attorney-client relationship in which the factual matters involved were so related to the facts in the pending litigation that it creates a genuine threat that confidences revealed to his former counsel will be divulged to his present adversary.").

[4] Rule 1.09 cmt. 4B.

[5] *See* Rule 1.06 cmt. 1; *Centerline Indus., Inc. v. Knize*, 894 S.W.2d 874, 876 (Tex. App.—Waco 1995, orig. proceeding) (stating that the substantial-relationship test implicates two separate duties: "the duty to preserve confidences and the duty of loyalty to a former client.").

[6] *Texaco, Inc. v. Garcia*, 891 S.W.2d 255, 256-57 (Tex. 1995) (quoting *NCNB Tex. Nat'l Bank v. Coker*, 765 S.W.2d 398, 400 (Tex. 1989)); *accord NCNB Tex. Nat'l Bank v. Coker*, 765 S.W.2d 398, 400 (Tex. 1989) ("The moving party must prove the existence of a prior attorney-client relationship in which the factual matters involved were so related to the facts in the pending litigation that it creates a genuine threat that confidences revealed to his former counsel will be divulged

The movant must produce "evidence of specific similarities capable of being recited in the disqualification order."[7]

Concerning what must be "similar" between the former representation and the current representation, some decisions talk about not only "factual matters," but also "subject matter, issues, and causes of action."[8] However, similarity of issues alone is

---

to his present adversary. Sustaining this burden requires evidence of specific similarities capable of being recited in the disqualification order.").

[7] *Ghidoni v. Stone Oak, Inc.*, 966 S.W.2d 573, 579 (Tex. App.—San Antonio 1998, pet. denied) (stating that "[i]n order to prove a substantial relationship between two matters, the movant must produce 'evidence of specific similarities capable of being recited in the disqualification order.'" (quoting *NCNB Tex. Nat'l Bank v. Coker*, 765 S.W.2d 398, 400 (Tex. 1989)).

[8] *Cimarron Agric., Ltd. v. Guitar Holding Co., L.P.*, 209 S.W.3d 197, 201 (Tex. App.—El Paso 2006, no pet.) ("A movant is not required to reveal any confidences, but must 'delineate with specificity the subject matter, issues and causes of action presented in [the] former representation.'") (quoting *J.K. & Susie L. Wadley Research Inst. & Blood Bank v. Morris*, 776 S.W.2d 271, 278 (Tex. App.—Dallas 1989, orig. proceeding)); *In re Drake*, 195 S.W.3d 232, 236 (Tex. App.—San Antonio 2006, orig. proceeding [mand. denied]); *Lopez v. Sandoval*, 2006 WL 417326, at *1 (Tex. App.—Corpus Christi-Edinburg 2006, no pet.) ("When contemplating whether disqualification of counsel is proper, the court must determine whether the matters embraced within the pending suit are *substantially related* to the factual matters involved in the previous suit. . . . The severity of the remedy of disqualification requires the movant to establish a preponderance of the facts indicating a substantial relation between the two representations. . . . The moving party must prove the existence of a prior attorney-client relationship in which the factual matters involved were so related to the facts in the pending litigation that it creates a genuine threat that confidences revealed to his former counsel will be divulged to his present adversary. . . . Sustaining this burden requires evidence of specific similarities capable of being recited in the disqualification order.") (citations omitted); *HECI Exploration Co. v. Clajon Gas Co.*, 843 S.W.2d 622, 627 (Tex. App.—Austin 1992, writ denied); *In re American Airlines, Inc.*, 972 F.2d 605, 614 (5th Cir. 1992), *cert. denied*, 113 S. Ct. 1262 (1993) (noting that, to establish a substantial relationship, a movant must delineate "with specificity the subject matters, issues and causes of action common to prior and current representations," and that the court must engage "in a painstaking analysis

not enough. Consider this example: a lawyer represents a multi-product corporate-client manufacturer in defense of product-liability claims involving aircraft engines; then that representation terminates, and later the lawyer sues the former client on a product-liability claim involving a garage door opener. The design-defect questions to the jury in the two cases might be identical, except for the factual difference in the products. Are those "substantially similar" matters? Probably not. A "genuine threat" of disclosure of relevant confidences would seem highly unlikely.

A related question arises in the context of purported "playbook" disqualifications. For instance, a lawyer may regularly represent a corporate client in a particular type of litigation, such as employment disputes. Over time, the lawyer may learn the client's general litigation and settlement strategies. If the representation of the corporate client ends, and the lawyer represents a former employee of the corporation on an employment claim, that preexisting knowledge may give the lawyer a practical advantage in handling the litigation and settlement. However, usually those facts alone do not show that the prior and subsequent matters are substantially similar.[9]

---

of the facts and precise application of precedent").

[9] *See, e.g., Capital City Church of Christ v. Novak,* 2007 WL 1501095 (Tex. App.—Austin 2007, no pet.) ("[A]n attorney's mere generalized knowledge of a client's 'inner workings' in regard to selecting experts or fact witnesses, 'preparing and responding to discovery requests, formulating defense strategies, trial preparation, and attending settlement conferences' [does not] constitute the required "specific factual similarities" between prior and subsequent representations); *In re Drake,* 195 S.W. 3d 232, 236-37 (Tex. App.—San Antonio 2006, orig. proceeding [mand. denied]) (holding that mere fact that lawyer had long represented county tax appraisal district in suits over valuation of property, involving similar defenses and strategies, did not establish "substantial relationship" with subsequent valuation dispute in which counsel represented property owner); Restatement § 132 cmt. d ("A lawyer might . . . have learned a former client's preferred approach to bargaining in settlement discussions or negotiating business points in a transaction, willingness or unwillingness to be deposed by an adversary, and financial ability to withstand extended litigation or contract

A key principle underlying the substantial-relationship standard is that courts must not compel the former client to disclose the very communications or facts that the former client seeks to protect. For that reason, showing only the substantial-relationship between the two matters is sufficient. The movant need not show an "actual disclosure" of confidential information.[10] To avoid that disclosure, the Texas Supreme Court has held that two conclusive, irrebuttable presumptions apply. The first is that "confidences and secrets were imparted to the attorney during the prior representation."[11] The second presumption is that "an attorney who has obtained confidential information shares it with other members of the attorney's firm, because of the interplay among lawyers who practice together."[12] Thus, the two presumptions serve to protect the moving

---

negotiations. Only when such information will be directly in issue or of unusual value in the subsequent matter will it be independently relevant in assessing a substantial relationship.").

[10] *In re EPIC Holdings, Inc.*, 985 S.W.2d 41, 51 (Tex. 1998) ("We have held that two matters are 'substantially related' within the meaning of Rule 1.09 when a genuine threat exists that a lawyer may divulge in one matter confidential information obtained in the other because the facts and issues involved in both are so similar.... An actual disclosure of confidences need not be proven; the issue is the existence of a genuine threat of disclosure because of the similarity of the matters."); *Grant v. Thirteenth Court of Appeals*, 888 S.W.2d 466, 467 (Tex. 1994) ("[A]ny rule focusing on actual disclosure would place a virtually insurmountable burden on the party seeking disqualification, since the only persons who know whether confidences were actually shared will generally be the very lawyers seeking to avoid disqualification.").

[11] *Phoenix Founders, Inc. v. Marshall*, 887 S.W.2d 831, 833 (Tex. 1994) (citing *NCNB Tex. Nat'l Bank v. Coker*, 765 S.W.2d 398, 400 (Tex. 1989)); *accord In re Columbia Valley Healthcare Syst., L.P.*, 320 S.W.3d 819, 824 (Tex. 2010) ("An attorney who has previously represented a client may not represent another person in a matter adverse to the former client if the matters are the same or substantially related. . . . If the lawyer works on a matter, there is an irrebuttable presumption that the lawyer obtained confidential information during representation.") (citations omitted).

[12] *Phoenix Founders, Inc. v. Marshall*, 887 S.W.2d 831, 834 (Tex. 1994) (citing *Petroleum Wholesale, Inc. v. Marshall*, 751 S.W.2d 295, 299 (Tex. App.—Dallas 1988, orig. proceeding)); *accord In re Columbia Valley Healthcare Syst., L.P.*, 320 S.W.3d 819, 824 (Tex. 2010) ("When the lawyer

party "from being forced to reveal the very confidences sought to be protected."[13]

§ 4.4 Disciplinary Rule 1.09(a)(2): Violation of Confidentiality.

Rule 1.09(a)(2) generally prohibits representation adverse to a former client in a matter if the representation "in reasonable probability" will "involve a violation of Rule 1.05," the client-confidentiality rule. This basis for disqualification overlaps with the Rule 1.09(a)(3) substantial-relationship test, but it is a separate and independent ground for disqualification.[14]

---

moves to another firm and the second firm is representing an opposing party in ongoing litigation, a second irrebuttable presumption arises; it is presumed that the lawyer will share the confidences with members of the second firm, requiring imputed disqualification of the firm."); *National Medical Enters., Inc v. Godbey*, 924 S.W.2d 123, 131 (Tex. 1996) ("The attorney's knowledge is imputed by law to every other attorney in the firm. There is, in effect, an irrebuttable presumption that an attorney in a law firm has access to the confidences of the clients and former clients of other attorneys in the firm.").

[13] *Phoenix Founders, Inc. v. Marshall*, 887 S.W.2d 831, 834 (Tex. 1994); *accord National Medical Enters., Inc v. Godbey*, 924 S.W.2d 123, 131 (Tex. 1996); Restatement, §132 cmt. d(iii) ("The substantial-relationship test avoids requiring disclosure of confidential information by focusing upon the general features of the matters involved and inferences as to the likelihood that confidences were imparted by the former client that could be used to adverse effect in the subsequent representation. The inquiry into the issues involved in the prior representation should be as specific as possible without thereby revealing the confidential client information itself or confidential information concerning the second client.").

[14] *See Clarke v. Ruffino*, 819 S.W.2d 947, 950 (Tex. App.—Houston [14th Dist.] 1991, orig. proceeding) (stating that "the substantial relationship test ... is not the only basis which now governs a trial court's determination as to whether an attorney should be disqualified. . . . Because of the 'or' strategically placed in this rule [1.09], there are now more than one bases [sic] for disqualification of an attorney. . . . Not only should an attorney be disqualified if he is working on the same or substantially related matter, but he should not represent a client if the representation may in reasonable probability involve a violation of the new rules governing confidentiality

Assume, for example, that several lawyers in a large firm personally represent a client in a matter, and then one of those lawyers leaves the firm, joins another firm, and undertakes representation against the former client in a new matter that is not the "same or substantially related" to the matter in which the lawyer previously represented the former client. Disqualification would not be appropriate under the substantial-relationship test under Rule 1.09(a)(3). But then assume that at the former firm, the lawyer was in the firm's litigation section, which held weekly luncheons in which members discussed pending cases. At one luncheon, another lawyer discussed and disclosed facts concerning a particular case she was handling and those facts are relevant to the new matter in which the former firm member is adverse to the former client. That unusual situation might raise a disqualifying conflict under Rule 1.09(a)(2) but not under Rule 1.09(a)(3).

Note that the definition of "confidential information" is very broad. It includes not only information protected by the attorney-client privilege, but also "all information relating to a client or furnished by the client . . . acquired by the lawyer during the course of or by reason of the representation of the client."[15] Rule 1.05 prohibits both unauthorized disclosures of confidential information (Rule 1.05(b)(1)) and improper use of such information to the disadvantage of the former client (Rule 1.05(b)(3)).

---

of information.") (citations omitted); *In re Roseland Oil & Gas, Inc.*, 68 S.W.3d 784, 787 (Tex. App.—Eastland 2001, orig. proceeding) (disqualifying lawyers who represented multiple defendants, then withdrew from representation of two defendants but continued to represent the other defendants and took positions adverse to their former clients, and concluding that disqualification was necessary under both Rule 1.09(a) (2) and (a) (3)); *Wasserman v. Black*, 910 S.W.2d 564, 568 (Tex. App.—Waco 1995, orig. proceeding) (disqualifying a lawyer under Rule 1.09(a) (2)).

[15] Rule 1.05(a).

§ 4.5 Disciplinary Rule 1.09(a)(1): Questioning Lawyer's Services or Work Product.

Rule 1.09(a)(1) generally prohibits a lawyer from undertaking representation adverse to a former client when the current client "questions the validity of the lawyer's services or work product for the former client." As Comment 3 to the Rule explains, the classic example is when a lawyer drafts a will leaving the testator's property to a designated beneficiary and then represents the heirs to contest the will.[16]

§ 4.6 Rule 1.09(b)-(c): Imputation of Conflicts of Interest.[17]

Rule 1.09(b) and Rule 1.09(c) address imputation issues. Generally, if Rule 1.09(a) prohibits one lawyer in a firm from representing a client adverse to a former client, then under Rule 1.09(b) no other lawyer in the firm may represent the client. The disqualification is firm-wide.

Comment 5 to the Rule addresses the extent of that imputation in two situations. First, a client may terminate a law firm's representation. Then the imputation of the former-client conflict bars representation of a new client adverse to the former client not only by the lawyer who personally represented the former client, but also by any other member of the firm, including lawyers who join the firm after the termination. Second, if a

---

[16] *See also In re Epic Holdings, Inc.*, 985 S.W.2d 41, 52 (Tex. 1998) (concluding that disqualification was necessary under both Rule 1.09(a)(1) and (a)(3)); *In re Basco*, 221 S.W.3d 637, 638 (Tex. 2007) (disqualifying a hospital's lawyer in a doctor's suit concerning termination of hospital privileges, when the doctor asserted that he had relied on the advice of lawyers in the firm, one of whose partners had joined the firm representing the hospital; stating that the "legal system's image is ill-served by lawyers criticizing the work of their former associates with whom they shared the fees paid for the work"; and noting that the lawyer might need to challenge the validity of former firm's legal advice).

[17] *See generally* Chapter 16, below, concerning imputation and screening.

lawyer in a firm personally represents a client and then leaves that law firm and joins another firm, and if Rule 1.09(a) prevents that lawyer from representing a client adverse to the former client, Rule 1.09(b) prohibits all other lawyers in the new firm from undertaking the representation.

Rule 1.09(c) addresses the situation in which the personally-prohibited lawyer leaves the firm. If no other lawyer in that firm personally represented the former client, the firm is free to represent a client against the former client—with two exceptions. The first exception is if the new representation would fall under the prohibition of Rule 1.09(a)(1). That means that if the firm's new client desires to challenge the "validity" of the services or work product that the firm provided for the former client, the firm must not represent the new client.

The second exception applies if the proposed new-client representation would violate Rule 1.09(a)(2)—that is, "in reasonable probability" the firm's representation of the new client would involve a violation of the firm's confidentiality obligation to the former client under Rule 1.05 (the confidential-information rule). Apart from those exceptions, when the personally-prohibited lawyer leaves, the firm generally is free to represent the new client even if the representation is adverse to the former client in a matter that is the same matter or a matter substantially related to the firm's representation of the former client. If the firm does not possess confidential information of the former client, and if the new representation does not question the firm's services or work product for the firm's former client, the firm may accept the representation adverse to the former client.

The Texas Supreme Court's Committee on Professional Ethics has issued several opinions attempting to explain those principles.[18] As

---

[18] *See, e.g.,* Tex. Comm. on Prof'l Ethics, Ops. 501, 527, 598. The State Bar Act provides that the Committee's opinions are not binding on the

the Committee summarized its view of the general standards in Opinion 527:

1. Rule 1.09 prohibits an attorney who has personally represented a former client from representing a person in a matter adverse to the former client if such new representation would violate any of the provisions of Rule 1.09(a).

2. If an attorney is prohibited under Rule 1.09(a) from accepting a representation adverse to a former client, each attorney currently associated with such disqualified attorney is vicariously prohibited from accepting such representation under Rule 1.09(b).

3. If an attorney who *personally* represented a former client leaves a law firm, the lawyers who remain at the firm are thereafter prohibited from knowingly representing a person adverse to that former client only if a lawyer presently associated with the firm is personally disqualified from accepting the representation under Rule 1.09(a) or the firm's proposed representation involves the validity of the departed lawyer's legal services or work product for such former client while he was associated with the firm, or the proposed representation will with reasonable probability involve a violation of Rule 1.05 with respect to the confidential information of

---

Texas Supreme Court. Tex. Gov't Code § 81.092(c); *see also Royston, Rayzor, Vickery & Williams, LLP v. Lopez*, 467 S.W.3d. 494, 503 (Tex. 2015) ("Opinions of the Professional Ethics Committee carry less weight than do the Disciplinary Rules as to legal obligations of attorneys, but they are nevertheless advisory as to those obligations."). Nonetheless, Texas practitioners and courts often consider and rely upon the Committee's opinions.

such former client.

4. If, as in this ethics opinion, a lawyer terminates his association with a law firm and such firm retains a client *personally* represented by a departing lawyer while that lawyer was associated with the firm, any subsequent representation by the departed lawyer adverse to such former client is governed by Rule 1.09(a). Additionally, all lawyers currently associated with the departed lawyer are treated the same by reason of Rule 1.09(b). The departed lawyer and members of his new firm can represent a person adverse to such former client only if the representation does not violate Rule 1.09(a) (1), (2), or (3).

§ 4.7 Rule 1.09(a): Personal Attorney-Client Relationship.

Apart from imputed disqualification under Rule 1.09(b)-(c), the Rule 1.09(a) prohibition against representation adverse to a former client applies only to a lawyer who "personally . . . formerly represented" the client. Comment 2 to the Rule recognizes that the issue of personal representation may involve "both questions of fact and law." The Comment specifically identifies as possibly relevant factors: "how the former representation actually was conducted within the firm; the nature and scope of the former client's contacts with the firm (including any restrictions the client may have placed on the dissemination of confidential information within the firm); and the size of the firm."

§ 4.8 Disqualification Exception: Client Consent.

As Rule 1.09(a) states, a former client generally may give "prior consent" to what otherwise would be a disqualifying former-client conflict. As a practical matter, of course, the consent need not be "prior." The former client may expressly consent after the new, adverse representation commences. Or the former client simply may decide to waive the issue and not object to the former counsel's adverse representation or seek disqualification or other remedies. Comment 10 to the Rule notes that to obtain a valid consent, the lawyer should disclose the "relevant circumstances, including the lawyer's past or intended role on behalf of each client, as appropriate."[19]

---

[19] See, e.g., *In re Cerberus Capital Mgt., L.P.*, 164 S.W3d 379, 382-83 (Tex. 2005) (holding that a consent to representation was valid and met the standards set out in Comment 10 to Rule 1.09); *Davis v. Stansbury*, 824 S.W.3d 278 (Tex. App.—Houston [1st Dist.] 1992, orig. proceeding) (holding that consent was invalid when the client did not receive adequate information). *See also* Chapter 17 concerning waiver by delay.

Chapter 5

Disciplinary Rule 1.06
Concurrent Conflict of Interests

§ 5.1 Introduction.

Disqualification of counsel under Rule 1.06, the general conflict-of-interest rule, occurs less often than under Rule 1.09, the former-client conflict rule. Rule 1.06 conflicts of interest are more likely to result in legal-malpractice or breach-of-fiduciary-duty claims than in motions to disqualify counsel. But disqualifications under Rule 1.06 standards do occur, and the standards merit close attention. These conflicts are sometimes referred to as "concurrent" conflicts of interest because most often they relate to situations in which conflicts arise in the representation of two or more current clients.[1]

Rule 1.06 generally prohibits representation involving these types of conflicts of interest:

1. Rule 1.06(a): representing opposing parties in the same case.

2. Rule 1.06(b)(1): representing a person if the representation involves a "substantially related matter" in which the person's interests are "materially and directly adverse" to the interests of another client of the lawyer or firm.

3. Rule 1.06(b)(2): representing a person if the

---

[1] By comparison, Model Rule 1.7 expressly provides that a "concurrent conflict of interest" exists if "(1) the representation of one client will be directly adverse to another client; or (2) there is a significant risk that the representation of one or more clients will be materially limited by the lawyer's responsibilities to another client, a former client or a third person or by a personal interest of the lawyer."

representation "reasonably appears to be" adversely limited by the lawyer's or firm's responsibilities to the interests of (1) another client, (2) a third person, or (3) the lawyer or firm.

4. Rule 1.06(d): representing any of the parties who are involved in a dispute among themselves arising out of a matter in which the lawyer previously represented the same parties.

§ 5.2 Rule 1.06(a): the prohibition against representing opposing parties in the same case.

Rule 1.06(a) prohibits lawyers from representing "opposing parties to the same litigation." As Comment 2 to the Rule explains, the phrase "opposing parties" contemplates a situation in which "a judgment favorable to one of the parties will directly impact unfavorably upon the other party."[2]

---

[2] *See* Tex. Comm. on Prof'l Ethics, Op. 635 ("It should be noted that because the lawyer in these circumstances has a lawyer-client relationship with a spouse in a divorce or related proceeding, the lawyer is not permitted to provide legal services to the other spouse in the same proceeding. Even though the lawyer's services with respect to a divorce may be limited in scope by agreement, a lawyer is not permitted to advise both spouses in a divorce proceeding since such spouses are adverse parties in a litigation matter. *See* Rule 1.06(a) of the Texas Disciplinary Rules of Professional Conduct . . . ."); *cf.* Op. 500 (addressing a lawyer's proposed representation of two persons injured in a single accident caused by a third person, when it became clear that the third person had limited funds to pay a possible judgment or settlement so that the limits were substantially less than the likely verdict range; and stating that "[a] lawyer may not represent opposing parties to the same litigation. [Rule 1.06(a).] Although co-plaintiffs, technically, are not opposing parties, Comment 2 states that the 'term "opposing parties" as used in this Rule contemplates a situation where a judgment favorable to one of the parties will directly impact unfavorably upon the other party.' Therefore, under the limited scope of the question presented, the more funds one party will receive from a limited amount of available funds to pay for a possible judgment or settlement, the less the other party will receive.").

§ 5.3 Rule 1.06(b): the substantially-related-matter and reasonable-appearance prohibitions.

Rule 1.06(b) has two prohibitions. The first is the substantially-related prohibition in Rule 1.06(b)(1):

> [A] lawyer shall not represent a person if the representation of that person . . . involves a substantially related matter in which that person's interests are materially and directly adverse to the interests of another client of the lawyer or the lawyer's firm.[3]

Comment 6 explains that the representation is "directly adverse" if,

> the lawyer's independent judgment on behalf of a client or the lawyer's ability or willingness to consider, recommend or carry out a course of action will be or is reasonably likely to be adversely affected by the lawyer's representation of, or responsibilities, to the other client . . . [or] if the lawyer reasonably appears to be called upon to espouse adverse positions in the same matter or a related matter.[4]

Rule 1.06(b)'s second prohibition, the adversely-limited prohibition in Rule 1.06(b)(2), applies if,

---

[3] *Cf. In re B.L.D.*, 113 S.W.3d 340, 346-47 (Tex. 2003) (in a case involving potential termination of parental rights, holding that Texas Family Code § 107.013(b) provides that indigent parents who are defendants in the same suit are entitled to nonconflicted counsel, and therefore, under Rule 1.06(b)(1), the trial court must determine whether a substantial risk exists that the appointed counsel's obligations to one parent would materially and adversely affect his or her obligations to the other parent).

[4] *See, e.g., Ray v. T.D.*, 2008 WL 341490 (Tex. App.—Austin 2008, no pet.) (concluding that a lawyer had a conflict of interest in representing competing claimants to limited settlement proceeds).

the representation . . . reasonably appears to be or become adversely limited by the lawyer's or law firm's responsibilities to another client or to a third person or by the lawyer's or law firm's own interests.

§ 5.4 Rule 1.06(c): consent; consentable and nonconsentable conflicts.

When a Rule 1.06(b) conflict exists, a lawyer may be able to undertake the conflicted representation if the clients or prospective clients consent. But not all conflicts are consentable. Rule 1.06(c)(1) states that the lawyer may seek consent only if the lawyer "reasonably believes the representation of each client will not be materially affected . . . ."

That reasonable-belief standard is objective. As Comment 7 to the Rule explains, "when a disinterested lawyer would conclude that the client should not agree to the representation under the circumstances, the lawyer involved should not ask for such agreement or provide representation based on the client's consent."[5]

---

[5] The Texas Committee on Professional Ethics has issued several opinions concluding that conflicts of interest were nonconsentable in various settings. *See, e.g.*, Op. 599 (addressing a situation in which lawyer served as a bail bondsman for a client and added to the court's bond form a provision having the client agree that if the client failed to appear at the court hearing, the lawyer could enter a no-contest plea that might result in issuance of an arrest warrant for the client); Op. 536 (addressing an arrangement under which a lawyer would receive a solicitation fee from an investment adviser for referring a client to the adviser); Op. 547 (analyzing a proposal for a group of medical professionals to fund a law firm's advertising, with the expectation that the firm would refer clients to the medical group); Op. 500 (addressing possible conflicts arising from a lawyer's joint representation in a personal injury case of both the driver and passenger who were in a car involved in an auto accident with another vehicle; and stating that "[i]f the extent of the negligence of the [client-]driver is such that the [client-]passenger should assert a cause of action against the driver of the automobile in which he or she was a passenger, dual representation

When a conflict of interest is consentable and a lawyer or firm desires to proceed with the conflicted representation, Rule 1.06(c)(2) requires that the lawyer obtain the clients' informed consent. Rule 1.06(c)(2) allows the lawyer to proceed with the representation if each affected or potentially affected client consents to the representation after "full disclosure of the existence, nature, implications, and possible adverse consequences of the common representation and the advantages involved, if any."

As Comment 8 emphasizes, the disclosure and consent "are not formalities." Arguments concerning the adequacy of disclosure are common in disqualification hearings, and Comment 8 also recognizes that the sufficiency of the disclosure may depend upon the sophistication of the client.

While the Texas Rules do not require that the disclosures or consent be in writing, Comment 8 also states that often it is "prudent" for the lawyer to provide the multiple clients with "at least a written summary of the considerations disclosed."[6] On the other hand, a personal, straightforward conversation with each client is sometimes the most practical way to communicate the substance of the sometimes complex and confusing conflict disclosures. However, an internal firm

---

may not be permissible (e.g. both drivers disregard the stop sign at a four-way stop intersection). In such a case, it is reasonable to assume that a disinterested lawyer would conclude that the client should not agree to dual representation. However, the circumstances of each case must be examined on a case by case basis. Such an examination is essential because notwithstanding the conflict, dual representation could be permitted under Rule 1.06(c) under a different set of circumstances (e.g. the passenger may be a family member of the driver, and after full disclosure, may not wish to assert a cause of action against the driver).").

[6] *See In re Cerberus Capital Mgt., L.P.*, 164 S.W.3d 379, 383 (Tex. 2005) (noting that when the law firm obtained oral consent from the client's general counsel, the procedure was "a permissible, albeit inadvisable, manner of providing disclosure and obtaining consent under the Disciplinary Rules").

memo that memorializes the disclosures and the key points disclosed can be helpful evidence in a later disqualification hearing or lawsuit.

In some instances, even if the conflict is theoretically consentable, the lawyer is unable to seek consent from all of the affected clients. For instance, if the lawyer represents different clients in related matters, one of the clients may refuse to permit the lawyer to disclose to the other client the information that would be necessary to obtain informed consent. In that situation, the lawyer must not seek consent from the other client.

In some conflict situations, only one client is involved—e.g., if the source of the conflict is the lawyer's or firm's own interests (Rule 1.06(b)(2)).[7]

While advanced-consent is sometimes effective, a broad, vague, open-ended consent usually is inadequate.[8] Moreover, the conflicts-checking process is not a one-time-forever snapshot. As a case or matter proceeds, new parties and

---

[7] *Cf. Bullard v. Chrysler Corp.*, 925 F. Supp. 1180 (E.D. Tex. 1996) (allowing a plaintiff's lawyer to withdraw from a product-liability suit; noting that the lawyer had written a letter to cocounsel stating, in a truly unfortunate mixed metaphor, that Chrysler "[has] me by the testicles. I cannot bite the hand that feeds me so well, especially since I have so many good Chrysler cases that are being held up due to [this case]"; and requiring the lawyer to pay a $2,500 fine and complete 10 hours of ethics CLE, and referring the lawyer to the State Bar).

[8] *See, e.g.,* Model Rule 1.7 cmt. 22 ("The effectiveness of such [advance] waivers is generally determined by the extent to which the client reasonably understands the material risks that the waiver entails. The more comprehensive the explanation of the types of future representations that might arise and the actual and reasonably foreseeable adverse consequence of those representations, the greater the likelihood that the client will have the requisite understanding. . . . If the consent is general and open-ended, then the consent ordinarily will be ineffective . . . ."). *See also* ABA Comm. on Ethics and Prof. Resp., Formal Op. 05-436 (2005) (addressing informed consent to future conflicts of interest).

issues may surface and new facts may develop that create unanticipated adversities. Those changing circumstances may require a lawyer to obtain additional informed consent.

In disqualification proceedings, it is not unusual for the parties to argue about the effectiveness of alleged consent. A common dispute is whether the lawyer provided "full disclosure" of all of the items required by Rule 1.06(c)(2): "the existence, nature, implications, and possible adverse consequences of the common representation and the advantages, if any." Usually the dispute focuses on whether the lawyer adequately explained all implications and possible adverse consequences of the conflict.

For example, in *In re Cerberus Capital Mgt., L.P.*,[9] the trial court disqualified a law firm, but the Texas Supreme Court overturned that result based on an oral consent, later confirmed in writing. The alleged conflict of interest was a former-client conflict under Rule 1.09, rather than a concurrent conflict under Rule 1.06, but the dispute concerning the adequacy of the consent was typical.[10] WSNet Holdings retained Vinson & Elkins (V&E) to prepare an asset purchase agreement concerning Classic Communications, Inc. Two days later, WSNet terminated the firm's work on the project. A year after that, a WSNet shareholder filed a shareholder derivative suit alleging that certain defendants had usurped WSNet's corporate opportunity to buy Classic Communications and other assets. Some of the defendants in that case contacted V&E regarding representation. A V&E lawyer then called WSNet's general counsel to seek consent to represent the

---

[9] 164 S.W.3d 379 (Tex. 2005).

[10] Rule 1.09(a) expressly permits representation in certain former-client situations if the lawyer or firm obtains "prior consent." Comment 10 to Rule 1.09 states that the "waiver" is effective only if "there is consent after disclosure of the relevant circumstances, including the lawyer's past or intended role on behalf of each client, as appropriate. *See* Comments 7 and 8 to Rule 1.06."

defendants, and disclosed "the factual basis of the potential conflict." The general counsel gave oral consent. V&E sent a confirming letter, which a WSNet vice president and chief financial officer signed. The letter stated, in part, that "I write to confirm that, as you stated during our conversation last week, you have agreed, on behalf of WSNet . . . to waive any conflict of interest arising from" the representation, and that "[a]fter full disclosure of relevant facts, you have consented to V&E representing the Defendants in the above-titled action." WSNet filed for bankruptcy protection, and the bankruptcy trustee moved to disqualify V&E, arguing that V&E's letter had not "fully and accurately" disclosed the conflict. The supreme court disagreed, and overturned the trial court's disqualification of counsel. The court stated that the initial oral consent was "a permissible, albeit inadvisable, manner of providing disclosure and obtaining consent under the Disciplinary Rules."[11]

§ 5.5 Rule 1.06(d): conflicts arising from prior representation of multiple clients in a matter.

Rule 1.06(d) applies when a lawyer represents multiple clients in a matter and then a dispute arises among the clients concerning the matter. In that situation, the Rule provides that the lawyer may not represent any of those parties unless the lawyer obtains "prior consent." However, as a practical matter, even without prior consent the lawyer could represent one or more of the parties if all of the parties agreed to waive the conflict.

---

[11] *See also Conoco Inc. v. Baskin*, 803 S.W.2d 416, 419-20 (Tex. App.—El Paso 1991, orig. proceeding) (concluding that the record failed to show consent that complied with Rule 1.06(c)); *MacFarlane v. Nelson*, 2005 WL 2240949, at *7 (Tex. App.—Austin 2005, pet denied) (holding that "[a]ny conflict of interest that existed for Nelson in representing both MacFarlane and Becker in the Steck I transaction was remedied by Nelson's reasonable belief that neither client would be materially affected and Nelson's disclosure followed by MacFarlane's consent.").

§ 5.6 Withdrawal from representation.

Rule 1.06(e) provides that if a lawyer has accepted representation in violation of Rule 1.06, the lawyer shall promptly withdraw from representing one or more clients as necessary to make the remaining representation proper. The same withdrawal requirement applies when a lawyer initially accepts the multiple representation properly, but a conflict develops and the representation becomes improper.[12] (Similarly, Rule 1.15(a)(1) requires that a lawyer must withdraw from representation if the representation will violate any rules of professional conduct or any other law.)

However, a Rule 1.06(e) withdrawal does not necessarily solve all of the conflict issues. When a lawyer withdraws from representing one of multiple clients, that client becomes a former client. The lawyer then must analyze the situation to determine if a former-client conflict exists under Rule 1.09.[13]

---

[12] *See, e.g., In re Posadas USA, Inc.*, 100 S.W.3d 254, 258-59 (Tex. App.— San Antonio 2001, orig. proceeding) (granting mandamus relief to require the trial court to grant a lawyer's motion to withdraw five days before trial, when one client gave him information that created a conflict under Rule 1.06(b)); *Ames v. Miller*, 184 F. Supp.2d 566, 576 (N.D. Tex. 2002) (noting that the court had concluded that the lawyers representing multiple plaintiffs-investors "could not ethically" represent certain members of the investor group who might have a claim against other members of the investor group, and that because of the "serious conflict of interest," had ordered that one of the three lawyers no longer represent two of the plaintiffs but instead represent other investors).

[13] *See, e.g., In re A.F.*, 51 S.W.3d 848, 849 (Tex. App.—Waco 2001, no pet.) (concluding that in a suit seeking to terminate the parental rights of two indigent parents who were represented by the same lawyer, the trial court had to conduct a hearing to determine if counsel had a conflict of interest; and stating that if, on remand, the trial court determined "that separate attorneys are required, it shall appoint them. Because of Rule 1.09 . . . regarding the representation of former clients, the trial court should inquire into whether [present counsel] is qualified for one of these appointments.").

§ 5.7 Imputation of Rule 1.06 conflicts.

Rule 1.06(f) has a simple, broad imputation provision. If Rule 1.06 prohibits a particular lawyer from undertaking or continuing representation, Rule 1.06(f) prohibits any "other lawyer while a member or associated with that lawyer's firm" from engaging in such conduct.[14]

---

[14] *See* Chapter 16, concerning imputation and screening.

Chapter 6

Disciplinary Rule 1.10

Successive Government and Private Employment

§ 6.1 Introduction.

Rule 1.10 addresses conflicts arising from successive government and private employment. The central goal of the Rule is to prevent a lawyer from "exploiting public office for the advantage of a private client."[1] The Rule generally focuses on five situations:

1. A former government lawyer who represents a private client concerning a matter in which the lawyer participated while in government.

2. A government lawyer who has confidential government information about a person and then represents a private client whose interests are adverse to that person.

3. A lawyer who represents a private client in a matter and then enters government service and participates in the same matter.

4. A government lawyer who negotiates for employment with a party (or a party's counsel) who is involved in a matter in which the government lawyer is participating.

5. A government lawyer who moves from one unit or level of government to another (e.g., from state to federal) and then represents the second government entity in a matter in which the lawyer participated

---

[1] Rule 1.10 cmt. 1.

for the first entity or concerning which the lawyer has confidential government information.

The Rule also addresses whether resulting conflicts are imputed to other lawyers in the firm or the government entity and when screening procedures will avoid imputation of conflicts.

§ 6.2 A former government lawyer who represents a private client.

Under Rule 1.10(a), a former "public officer or employee" generally must not represent a private client in a matter in which the lawyer participated "personally and substantially" as a government lawyer.[2] An exception applies if the government agency "consents after consultation."[3]

When a lawyer in a law firm is subject to the prohibition in Rule 1.10(a), then Rule 1.10(b) imputes the conflict and the prohibition against representation to the other lawyers in the same firm. A firm can avoid the imputed conflict if it satisfies three requirements:

1. The lawyer who is personally subject to the Rule 1.10(a) disqualification must be "screened" from any participation in the matter.[4] The Rule does not define screening, but Comment 3 explains that the screened lawyer must not (a) furnish other lawyers (or presumably staff) "information relating to the matter," (b) have access to the files, or (c) participate or advise concerning the matter.

2. The personally affected lawyer must not be "apportioned" any part of the fee from the

---

[2] Rule 1.10(a).

[3] *Id.*

[4] Rule 1.10(b)(1).

representation.[5] (However, Comment 5 states that the lawyer may receive a "salary or partnership share" under an independent, preexisting agreement.)

3. The government agency must receive reasonably prompt written notice. Comment 6 to the Rule explains that the lawyer must give notice "as soon as practicable," but that the lawyer need not make a "premature disclosure" that would injure the client. The agency must have a "reasonable opportunity" to ascertain compliance with Rule 1.10 and to take appropriate action.

§ 6.3 A former government lawyer who has confidential government information.

Rule 1.10(c) prohibits representation when a former government lawyer has certain confidential government information:

1. The lawyer acquired the information while the lawyer was a public officer or employee.

2. The information is about an entity or person who would be adverse to a private client of the lawyer.[6] (Rule 1.10(h) defines "private client" to include both a private party and a government agency if

---

[5] *Id.*

[6] *See Smith v. Abbott,* 311 S.W.3d 62, 76 (Tex. App.—Austin 2010, pet. denied) (concluding that when a lawyer had worked in the Office of Attorney General as an administrative law judge in the Child Support Division to decide license suspension proceedings brought to enforce child-support obligations, and later the lawyer allegedly used confidential government information that he had acquired in that position to identify and solicit clients to challenge the authority of the State Office of Administrative Hearings to conduct license-suspension hearings, the Rule 1.10(c) prohibition did not apply because he was not using the information for a client who was "adverse" to those persons).

the lawyer is not a public officer or employee of the agency.)

3. The lawyer knows or should know that the information is confidential. Rule 1.10(g) provides a three-part definition of "confidential information": (a) the information was obtained under governmental authority; (b) the information is not otherwise available to the public; and (c) at the time the Rule is applied, either the law prohibits the government from disclosing the information to the public or the government has a legal privilege not to disclose the information.[7]

When a law firm learns that the Rule 1.10(c) disqualification applies to one lawyer in a firm, the firm and other lawyers in the firm must not represent the private client unless the disqualified lawyer is screened from participation in the matter and is "apportioned no part of the fee."[8]

§ 6.4 A lawyer who moves from private practice to government employment.

Under Rule 1.10(e)(1), a lawyer who moves from private practice to a position as public officer or employee shall not participate in a matter involving a private client if the lawyer had represented that client in the same matter while in private practice.[9] An exception applies if the law does not authorize

---

[7] See, e.g., Smith v. Abbott, 311 S.W.3d 62, 75 (Tex. App.—Austin 2010, pet. denied) (holding that information that the Attorney General's Office maintained concerning license-suspension proceedings to enforce child-support obligations was confidential).

[8] See Rule 1.10(d) & cmts. 3-5.

[9] See Tex. Comm. on Prof'l Ethics, Op. 538 (2001) (ruling that a lawyer who served as criminal defense counsel in a proceeding, and who then was elected district attorney, would be prohibited from prosecuting a motion to revoke probation arising from the same matter.).

anyone else to act in place of the lawyer. The Rule does not impute the disqualification to other lawyers in the agency.[10] The Rule does not require screening of the lawyer, but Comment 9 to the Rule indicates that "sound practice" is to screen the lawyer to the extent feasible.

§ 6.5 A government lawyer who negotiates for private employment.

Rule 1.10(e)(2) prohibits a lawyer who is serving as a public officer or employee from negotiating for private employment with a party or lawyer in a matter that the government lawyer is participating in "personally and substantially."

§ 6.6 A lawyer who moves from one government agency to another.

Rule 1.10(i) addresses the situation involving a lawyer who moves from "one body politic" to another. Comment 10 to the Rule explains that "one body politic" refers to one "unit or level of government," such as the federal government, state government, county, or city. However, the term does not include agencies within the same unit of government—for example, a move from one state agency to another. When a lawyer moves from one body politic to another, the lawyer is subject to the representation restrictions in Rule 1.10(a)[11] and the confidential-government-information restrictions in Rule 1.10(c),[12] just as if the second body politic were a private client. The lawyer is also subject to the representation and employment-negotiation restrictions in Rule 1.10(e).[13]

---

[10] Rule 1.10 cmt. 9.

[11] *See* § 6.2, above.

[12] *See* § 6.3, above.

[13] *See* §§ 6.4 and 6.5, above.

Chapter 7

Disciplinary Rule 1.11

Adjudicatory Official or Law Clerk

§ 7.1 Introduction.

Rule 1.11 generally addresses two conflict-of-interest issues involving adjudicatory officials and law clerks: (1) representation of a client by a former adjudicatory official or law clerk concerning a matter in which the official or clerk participated; and (2) employment negotiations by an adjudicatory official or law clerk. Structurally, the Rule is similar to Rule 1.10.[1] Both rules focus on personal-and-substantial participation by the adjudicatory official or law clerk, provide a consent exception, and impose limited imputed disqualification.

The term "adjudicatory official" includes judges, special masters, referees, hearing officers, "comparable officials serving on tribunals," and "parajudicial officers."[2]

§ 7.2 A former judge or law clerk in private practice.

Rule 1.11(a) prohibits a lawyer from representing a client concerning a matter in which the lawyer "passed upon the merits or otherwise participated personally and substantially"

---

[1] *See* generally Chapter 6, above.

[2] *See* Rule 1.11 cmt. 2. *See also* Tex. Disciplinary R. Prof'l Conduct, Preamble: Terminology. The Preamble defines "adjudicatory official" as a person who serves on a "tribunal," which the Preamble then defines as "any governmental body or official or any other person engaged in a process of resolving a particular dispute or controversy," including mediators, hearing officers, and "comparable persons empowered to resolve or recommend a resolution of a particular matter."

as an "adjudicatory official" or law clerk.[3] The Rule provides a consent exception: if all parties consent "after disclosure," the lawyer may undertake the representation.

The trigger for the prohibition in Rule 1.11(a) is personal and substantial participation. Comment 1 identifies two situations that do not meet that standard. The first applies to a former judge on a multi-member court who did not participate in a particular matter that was pending before the court. The former judge may represent a client concerning the matter.[4] The second situation applies when a former judge exercised only administrative responsibility concerning the matter. As long as the former judge exercised only "remote or incidental administrative responsibility that did not affect the merits," the subsequent representation of the client would be permissible.[5]

Rule 1.11(c) provides for imputed disqualification. If a former adjudicatory official or law clerk is disqualified under Rule 1.11(a), then other lawyers in the firm must not knowingly represent the client unless the firm satisfies three screening requirements:

1. The personally disqualified lawyer is screened. Rule 1.11 does not define screening, but presumably the same concepts discussed in Comment 3 to Rule 1.10 apply.[6]

2. The lawyer must not be "apportioned" any part of the fee from the matter.[7]

---

[3] Comment 3 to the Rule notes that the Rule 1.11(a) prohibition applies to a lawyer even if the lawyer was not licensed at the time of service as a law clerk.

[4] Rule 1.11 cmt. 1.

[5] *Id.*

[6] See the discussion in § 6.2, above.

[7] *Cf.* Rule 1.10 cmt. 5, and the discussion in § 6:2, above.

3. The other parties in the proceeding must receive prompt written notice.[8]

In *In re de Brittingham*,[9] the court of appeals disqualified a former appellate court justice and her law firm under Rule 1.11. The opinion discussed various issues concerning Rule 1.11 disqualification standards, including the meaning of the terms "matter" and "consent" after disclosure, and whether disqualification under the Rule requires a showing of prejudice.

Brittingham involved probate proceedings. The disqualification motion sought to remove a former justice of the San Antonio Court of Appeals, Sarah Duncan and the members of her law firm. While a judge, Duncan had participated on a panel that affirmed two trial court orders from the same ancillary probate proceeding as the current probate proceeding. Duncan and her firm argued that those earlier appeals did not concern the same "matter," and that each separate appeal was a discrete matter. The court of appeals disagreed. The court pointed out while Rule 1.11 does not define "matter," Rule 1.10(f) does define that term, and the court relied on that definition. The court pointed out that the underlying ancillary proceeding had given rise to 14 appeals and original proceedings. The court also concluded that a single probate proceeding "consists of a continuing series of events" involving multiple, appealable orders on discrete issues. "Nonetheless, these discreet appealable issues arise from one probate proceeding."[10] Thus, the court held that "in this particular case the 'matter' is the ancillary probate proceeding and not each discrete appeal or original proceeding."[11]

Duncan and her firm also argued that the parties had consented,

---

[8] *Cf.* Rule 1.10 cmt. 6.

[9] 319 S.W.3d 95 (Tex. App.—San Antonio 2010, orig. proceeding)

[10] *Id.* at 99.

[11] *Id.*

within the meaning of Rule 1.11(a), in two ways. First, Duncan's name had appeared on the appellate brief filed in the matter. Second, the opposing parties had not objected to Duncan and her firm substituting as counsel for relators. On the first issue, the court of appeals concluded that merely listing Duncan's name on the brief was insufficient to constitute "consent after disclosure." Instead, "disclosure requires the lawyer to inform the party that she participated in the matter personally and substantially as an adjudicatory official."[12] On the second issue, the court of appeals pointed out that when the opposing parties indicated they did not oppose substitution of counsel, they were unaware of Duncan's participation in the earlier appeal in the case and that the motion to substitute had not disclosed that participation. Consequently, that fact also failed to show consent after disclosure.[13]

Finally, the court of appeals rejected the argument that under Rule 1.11(a) the movants had to show prejudice. One of the decisions that Duncan and her firm relied on was *In re Sanders*,[14] but the court of appeals pointed out that that decision involved disqualification under Rule 3.08 (the lawyer-as-witness rule), and that the Comment to Rule 3.08 expressly refers to a showing of actual prejudice. Similarly, the other case that Duncan and her firm relied on was *In re Nitla S.A. de C.V.*[15] That decision did not address Rule 1.11. It involved a motion to disqualify a lawyer who had reviewed privileged documents that he received from the trial court. The Texas Supreme Court had concluded that no disciplinary rule expressly addressed that fact setting. Thus, the supreme court had formulated a new test specific to apply in that context. The court of appeals concluded that "[t]o require the party seeking disqualification under Rule 1.11 to show prejudice would

---

[12] *Id.* at 100.

[13] *Id.*

[14] 153 S.W.3d 54 (Tex. 2004).

[15] 92 S.W.3d 419 (Tex. 2002).

likely place an unattainable burden on that party because the party seeking disqualification does not know what insight an adjudicatory official has gained about the underlying case. . . . Requiring [the movant] to show that the confidential discussions among appellate court justices prejudiced him would be an impossible burden, and one we do not believe the rule does or should impose."[16]

§ 7.3 A judge or law clerk negotiating for employment.

Rule 1.11(b) addresses job negotiations by adjudicatory officials and law clerks. The Rule prohibits an adjudicatory official from negotiating for employment with any party or any party's counsel in a pending matter in which the adjudicatory official participates "personally and substantially."[17] However, the Rule treats law clerks differently: a law clerk may negotiate for employment after giving notice to the adjudicatory official.

---

[16] *Id.* at 100-01.

[17] *See* Tex. Comm. on Prof'l Ethics, Op. 583 (2008) (concluding that a lawyer may not agree to serve both as a mediator between parties in a divorce and as a lawyer to prepare the divorce decree and other necessary documents to effect an agreement resulting from the mediation because the arrangement would violate the Rule 1.11(b) employment-negotiation prohibition).

Chapter 8

Disciplinary Rule 3.08

Lawyer As Witness

§ 8.1 Introduction.

Motions to disqualify counsel based upon a lawyer acting as both a witness and advocate are quite common. But usually the motions fail because the targeted lawyer is not a "witness necessary to establish an essential fact," as required by Rule 3.08(a). As with most disqualification grounds, that determination is usually fact-specific.

Rule 3.08 is the "Lawyer as Witness" rule. It generally addresses three situations: (1) when a lawyer is a witness for the lawyer's client [paragraph (a)]; (2) when a lawyer will provide testimony "substantially adverse" to the client [paragraph (b)]; and (3) when another lawyer in the disqualified lawyer's firm may act as an advocate in the case when the client provides "informed consent" [paragraph (c)].[1]

Because of the potential for abuse in this type of disqualification, courts require the party seeking disqualification to show "actual prejudice."

Issues frequently arising under a lawyer-as-witness disqualification motion include:

---

[1] *See also* Rule 1.15(a)(1) (generally providing that a lawyer shall withdraw from representation if "the representation will result in violation of Rule 3.08 . . . .").

- Under paragraph (a):

  o Whether the targeted lawyer is a "necessary" witness to establish an "essential" fact for the client.

  o Whether one of the five exceptions under paragraph (a) applies, to permit the lawyer to serve as both advocate and witness.

- Under both paragraphs (a) and (b):

  o Whether the party seeking disqualification can show "actual prejudice."

- Under paragraph (c):

  o The extent to which the disqualified lawyer may continue to represent the client without violating the active-role prohibition.

§ 8.2 Rule 3.08 as a disqualification standard.

In general, courts refer to Rule 3.08 in determining lawyer-as-witness disqualification motions. While Comment 9 to the Rule emphasizes that the Rule sets out a "disciplinary standard" and is "not well suited as a standard" for disqualification, Comment 10 states that the Rule "may furnish some guidance" in disqualification proceedings "where the party seeking disqualification can demonstrate actual prejudice to itself resulting from the opposing lawyer's service in the dual roles." Comment 10 also cautions against using the rule as a "tactical weapon" to deprive a party of counsel of choice.[2] As that Comment further explains, allowing a lawyer

---

[2] As discussed in § 2.2 above, a meritorious disqualification motion may have proper, legitimate "tactical" advantage. *Cf.* Texas Lawyer's Creed, Art. III.19 ("I will not seek . . . disqualification unless it is necessary

to "unnecessarily" call opposing counsel as a witness would "subvert [the Rule's] true purpose by converting it into a mere tactical weapon in litigation." Texas appellate decisions reflect that ambivalence by cautioning against tactical abuse and by requiring a showing of actual prejudice[3]—but then also closely analyzing and applying the standards expressed in the Rule.[4]

Disqualification motions based on Rule 3.08 often fail on the actual-prejudice requirement.[5] Some opinions hold that trial courts should consider less severe remedies, before disqualification.[6]

---

for protection of my client's lawful objectives or is fully justified by the circumstances.").

[3] *See, e.g., Spears v. Fourth Court of Appeals*, 797 S.W.2d 654, 658 (Tex. 1990) ("While this rule is not intended as a standard for procedural disqualification, it may provide guidance in those cases in which the movant can demonstrate actual prejudice as a result of the dual roles of lawyer and witness. The comments, however, vehemently discourage the use of motions to disqualify as tactical weapons, as well as the unnecessary calling of an opponent's lawyer as a witness to invoke the rule's prohibition.") (citations omitted); *Ayres v. Canales*, 790 S.W.2d 554, 557-58 (Tex. 1990) (quoting Comment 10 and stating that to avoid misuse, a trial court "should require the party seeking disqualification to demonstrate actual prejudice to itself resulting from the opposing lawyer's service in the dual roles.").

[4] *See, e.g., Anderson Producing v. Koch Oil Co.*, 929 S.W.2d 416, 422 (Tex. 1996) ("Although Rule 3.08 was not promulgated as the controlling standard for disqualification proceedings, we have recognized that it articulates relevant considerations for such proceedings. While we do not exclude the possibility that we would apply a different standard under other appropriate circumstances, we decline to do so here when it has not been urged by the parties, either in this Court or below."); *In re Bahn*, 13 S.W.3d 865, 872 (Tex. App.—Fort Worth 2000, orig. proceeding) ("If the parties believe that a higher standard should be applied, they should offer countervailing considerations as to why the disciplinary rules should not be employed.").

[5] *See, e.g., Ayres v. Canales*, 790 S.W.2d 554, 557-58 (Tex. 1990); *In re Williard Law Firm, L.P.*, 2013 WL 4779691, *2 (Tex. App.—Houston [1st Dist.] 2013, orig. proceeding); *In re Sandoval*, 308 S.W.3d 31, 34 (Tex. App.—San Antonio 2009, orig. proceeding); *In re Frost*, 2008 WL 2122597, *3-4 (Tex. App.—Tyler 2008, orig. proceeding).

[6] *See, e.g., In re Fulp*, 2008 WL 1822758, *3 (Tex. App.—Corpus Christi

§ 8.3 Policy considerations for the lawyer-as-witness prohibition.

In deciding whether to disqualify a lawyer in the lawyer-as-witness context, courts sometimes analyze the policy considerations underlying the prohibition. Those considerations vary depending on whether the testimony would be on behalf of the client (paragraph (a)) or adverse to the client (paragraph (b)). As Comment 4 to the Rule states, in most situations the "principal concern" when a lawyer acts as both advocate and witness for a client is the "possible confusion" those dual roles can create for the fact finder. Ordinarily, of course, the risk of confusion is greater in a jury trial.[7] Allowing a lawyer to serve in the dual roles can "prejudice the opposing party" because while a witness testifies from personal knowledge, a lawyer-as-advocate explains and comments on evidence given by others.[8] "It may not be clear whether a statement by an advocate-witness should be taken as proof or as an analysis of proof."[9]

2008, orig. proceeding) (stating that the trial court should have considered "less severe means of remedying the perceived problems" with the lawyer's affidavit, such as striking the affidavit); *In re Bahn*, 13 S.W.3d 865, 876-77 (Tex. App.—Fort Worth 2000, orig. proceeding) (stating that when an issue arose concerning whether the lawyer, by testifying, might violate Rule 3.04(b), which prohibits a lawyer from paying a witness contingent on the outcome of the case, "the trial court should have considered less drastic measures besides disqualification to avoid possible rule 3.04 violations, such as giving Broussard and Phelps an opportunity to change their method of billing"); *In re McDaniel*, 2006 WL 408397, *3 (Tex. App.—Waco 2006, orig. proceeding) (stating that the movant had to demonstrate "actual prejudice" rather than just a "potential for prejudice," and had to show that the "trial court lacks any lesser means" to remedy potential harm).

[7] *See, e.g., In re Stone*, 2013 WL 1844267, *2 (Tex. App.—Houston [14th Dist] April 19, 2013, orig. proceeding) (noting that because the trial would be "a bench trial, the risk of confusion cannot simply be presumed.").

[8] Rule 3.08 cmt. 4.

[9] *Id.*

On the other hand, when a lawyer may provide testimony adverse to the client—the situation addressed in Rule 3.08(b)—a "substantial likelihood" exists that the adverse testimony will "damage the lawyer's ability to represent the client effectively."[10]

Texas decisions and ethics opinions also have considered these policy considerations:

- The potential difficulty for an opposing party to challenge the credibility of a testifying lawyer.

- The possibly reduced effectiveness of a testifying lawyer as a witness because the lawyer may be impeachable for self-interest and because of the client's interest in the outcome.

- The difficulty, and possible appearance of impropriety, when the lawyer has to argue or defend his credibility.

- The limitations, or at least awkwardness, for the lawyer who might need to consult with the client while testifying—e.g., consultation concerning attorney-client privilege issues.

- The difficulty and confusion if the lawyer both testifies and objects to questions by the opposing party.[11]

---

[10] Rule 3.08 cmt. 3.

[11] *See, e.g., In re Guidry*, 316 S.W.3d 729, 738 (Tex. App.—Houston [14th Dist] 2010, orig. proceeding); *Flores v. State*, 155 S.W.3d 144, 148 (Tex. Crim. App. 2004) (also adopting a "compelling-need" test that a prosecutor must meet before calling defense counsel as a witness); *Schwager v. Texas Commerce Bank, N.A.*, 813 S.W.2d 225, 227 (Tex. App.—Houston [1st Dist.] 1991, no writ); Tex. Comm. on Prof'l Ethics, Op. 471 (1992), Op. 468 (1991).

§ 8.4 Testimony on behalf of a client—Rule 3.08(a).

Rule 3.08(a) sets out the lawyer-as-witness prohibition when a lawyer may testify on behalf of a client. The Rule provides:

> (a) A lawyer shall not accept or continue employment as an advocate before a tribunal in a contemplated or pending adjudicatory proceeding if the lawyer knows or believes that the lawyer is or may be a witness necessary to establish an essential fact on behalf of the lawyer's client, unless:
>
>> (1) the testimony relates to an uncontested issue;
>>
>> (2) the testimony will relate solely to a matter of formality and there is no reason to believe that substantial evidence will be offered in opposition to the testimony;
>>
>> (3) the testimony relates to the nature and value of legal services rendered in the case;
>>
>> (4) the lawyer is a party to the action and is appearing pro se; or
>>
>> (5) the lawyer has promptly notified opposing counsel that the lawyer expects to testify in the matter and disqualification of the lawyer would work substantial hardship on the client.

Texas court decisions concerning disqualification under Rule 3.08(a) standards most often focus on the issue of whether the lawyer would be a "necessary witness" to establish an "essential fact." Texas appellate courts have frequently concluded that the evidence does not meet that necessary-witness standard.[12] Nonetheless, movants have sometimes satisfied the standard.[13]

Of the five exceptions to the general prohibition in Rule 3.08(a) against a lawyer acting as both advocate and witness on behalf of a client, paragraph (a)(5) is the most litigated in disqualification proceedings.[14] It has two requirements: (1) the

---

[12] *See, e.g., In re Sanders*, 153 S.W.3d 54, 57 (Tex. 2004) (concluding that the movant "fails to explain why other sources revealed in the record, such as [the husband's] own testimony or [the lawyer's] billing records, are insufficient to establish the nature and extent of" the obligation created by a barter arrangement between the husband and his lawyer); *In re Stone*, 2013 WL 1844267, at *2 n.1 (Tex. App.—Houston [14th Dist.] 2013, orig. proceeding) (stating that "[t]he attempt to . . . disqualify relator's attorney on the basis she took photographs smacks of gamesmanship."); *In re Estate of Arizola*, 401 S.W.3d 664, 673-74 (Tex. App.—San Antonio 2013, pet. denied) (noting that the movant-heir who sought to disqualify the administrator's lawyer alleged only that the lawyer "may" be called as a witness and did not identify any "essential fact" concerning which the lawyer would testify); *In re Hormachea*, 2004 WL 2597447, at *3 (Tex. App.—San Antonio 2004, orig. proceeding) (holding that movant failed to establish attorney's testimony was "necessary" or involved "essential facts"); *In re Leyendecker*, 2012 WL 3224108, *3 (Tex. App.—Houston [1st Dist.] 2012, orig. proceeding) (stating that movant "made no showing below and makes no argument in this original proceeding that any testimony [the attorney] could provide is not available from another source."). See also the discussion below in § 9.2 concerning the actual-prejudice requirement, and the discussion above in § 8.6 concerning another lawyer in the firm taking over the role as advocate and the lawyer-witness's continued involvement in the matter in a non-advocate role.

[13] *See, e.g., Mauze v. Curry*, 861 S.W.2d 869, 870 (Tex. 1993) (disqualifying a lawyer who represented a plaintiff in a legal malpractice case and who signed an affidavit presented in opposition to a motion for summary judgment); *In re Guidry*, 316 S.W.3d 729, 737-41 (Tex. App.—Houston [14th Dist.] 2010, orig. proceeding).

[14] *See, e.g., In re Guidry*, 316 S.W.3d 729, 740 n.14 (Tex. App.—Houston [14th Dist.] 2010, orig. proceeding) (concluding that the Rule 3.08(a)(5) exception was inapplicable because the lawyer did not give the required notice or meet the substantial-hardship requirement); *In re Bahn*, 13 S.W.3d 865, 874 (Tex. App.—Fort Worth 2000, orig. proceeding) (holding that the Rule 3.08(a)(5) exception did not apply when the lawyer did not send notice that he expected to testify until three days after the opposing party filed a motion to disqualify). Concerning other exceptions, see *Ogu v. C.I.A. Services, Inc.*, 2011 WL 947008, at *5 (Tex. App.—

lawyer must give prompt notice to opposing counsel that the lawyer "expects to testify"; (2) disqualification would cause "substantial hardship" for the client. The exception seeks to balance the interests of the client and opposing party.[15] The applicability of this exception often depends on the timeliness of the parties' actions. The testifying lawyer who seeks to rely on this exception cannot manufacture substantial hardship by deliberate delay in giving notice to the opposing party.[16] Likewise, after receiving notice, the opposing party should respond "at the earliest opportunity."[17]

§ 8.5 Testimony adverse to a client—Rule 3.08(b).

Rule 3.08(b) sets out the lawyer-as-witness prohibition that applies when a lawyer may give testimony adverse to a client.[18] The Rule provides:

A lawyer shall not continue as an advocate in a

Houston [1st Dist.] 2011, no pet.) (holding that Rule 3.08(a)(3) allowed a lawyer to act as counsel and to testify as an expert on attorney's fees); *Ayres v. Canales*, 790 S.W.2d 554, 557-58 (Tex. 1990, orig. proceeding) (holding that under Rule 3.08(a)(4) the trial court improperly disqualified a lawyer who represented himself in a suit concerning a referral fee); *cf. Health & Tennis Corp. of Am. v. Jackson*, 928 S.W.2d 583, 591 (Tex. App.—San Antonio 1996, writ dism'd w.o.j.), *overruled on other grounds, Southwestern Refining Co. v. Bernal*, 22 S.W.3d 425, 434-35 (Tex. 2000) (in a class action suit, holding that the trial court properly refused to disqualify a lawyer who testified at a class-certification hearing concerning the size of the class, and stating that the testimony related solely to the procedural issue of whether the lawsuit should be certified as a class. "This is a matter of formality under the disciplinary rule, and no substantial evidence was offered in opposition to the testimony.").

[15] *See* Rule 3.08 cmt. 7.

[16] *Id.*

[17] *Id.*

[18] *See, e.g., In re Hormachea*, 2004 WL 2597447, at *3-4 (Tex. App.—San Antonio 2004, orig. proceeding) (overturning the trial court's decision to disqualify a lawyer who had participated in a news conference at which some allegedly defamatory statements were made, and holding that the movants had not demonstrated that the lawyer's testimony would be adverse to his client).

pending adjudicatory proceeding if the lawyer believes that the lawyer will be compelled to furnish testimony that will be substantially adverse to the lawyer's client, unless the client consents after full disclosure.

As Comment 3 to the Rule recognizes, if a lawyer both acts as advocate and gives testimony that is "substantially adverse" to the client, a "substantial likelihood" exists that the situation will damage the lawyer's ability to represent the client effectively. While lawyers should try to avoid that situation, sometimes a lawyer can represent the client effectively despite providing adverse testimony. For example, the testimony may be "substantially adverse" but relate to a relatively minor issue in the case. Usually the problem arises when the case is well underway, and the lawyer's withdrawal would damage the client more than the adverse testimony.

The Rule also requires informed client consent before the lawyer may continue representation.

§ 8.6 Participation of other lawyers in a disqualified lawyer's firm—Rule 3.08(c).

Even if a lawyer is disqualified from acting as an advocate under Rule 3.08, Rule 3.08(c) permits another lawyer in the disqualified lawyer's firm to act as advocate for the client, if the client gives informed consent. Thus, if paragraphs (a) or (b) would prohibit one lawyer in the firm from acting as advocate before a tribunal, the firm may seek informed consent to permit another lawyer in the firm to take over that role.[19]

---

[19] *See, e.g., In re Acevedo*, 956 S.W.2d 770, 774 (Tex. App.—San Antonio 1997, orig. proceeding) (overturning disqualification of a lawyer who had joined a firm after the operative events, and stating that "disqualification of an attorney who is or may be a witness does not disqualify other attorneys in that attorney's law firm, provided the client's informed consent is obtained."); *cf.* Tex. Comm. on Prof'l Ethics, Op. 471 (1991) (ruling that

§ 8.7 Participation of a disqualified lawyer-witness in a role other than in-court advocate—Rule 3.08(c).

The prohibitions in Rule 3.08(a) and (b) focus on a lawyer acting as an "advocate." Paragraph (a) applies to a lawyer acting as an "advocate before a tribunal," and paragraph (b) applies to a lawyer acting as "advocate in a pending adjudicatory proceeding."[20] Then Rule 3.08(c) refers to the personally prohibited lawyer not taking an *"active* role *before the tribunal* in the presentation of the matter." Comment 8 to the Rule clarifies that the lawyer-witness may participate in "preparation of a matter for presentation to a tribunal." As the Texas Supreme Court stated in *Anderson Producing Inc. v. Koch Oil Co.,*[21] Rule 3.08 prohibits a testifying lawyer only from "acting as an advocate before a tribunal, not from engaging in pretrial, out-of-court matters, such as preparing and signing pleadings, planning trial strategy and pursuing settlement negotiations."[22]

---

when a lawyer in a firm testified in a trial, another lawyer in the firm could handle the appeal of the case if the client gave informed consent).

[20] The terminology section of the Preamble to the Rules defines "Tribunal" to include, among other things, "any governmental body or official or any other person engaged in a process of resolving a particular dispute or controversy." The definition of "adjudicatory proceeding," in turn, "denotes the consideration of a matter by a Tribunal."

[21] 929 S.W.2d 416, 422 (Tex. 1996).

[22] *See also Spain v. Montalvo,* 921 S.W.2d 852, 857 (Tex. App.—San Antonio 1996, orig. proceeding) (stating that a lawyer-witness "may still assist his client in preparation for trial.").

Chapter 9

Joint Defense Agreements

§ 9.1 Introduction.

Joint defense agreements are common in multi-party litigation. Defendants frequently agree to cooperate with one another and to keep certain information confidential. The Texas Supreme Court has made clear that a joint-defense agreement can provide a basis for disqualification, even in favor of a defendant that the lawyer has not personally represented.

§ 9.2 Disqualification standard.

The leading Texas decision on joint-defense-agreement disqualification is *National Medical Enters., Inc. v. Godbey.*[1] In *Godbey*, the Texas Supreme Court disqualified Baker & Botts from representing a client based on a joint-defense agreement that one of the firm's lawyers had signed before joining Baker & Botts. Criminal investigations and civil suits had targeted the NME group of companies concerning alleged patient mistreatment and fraudulent billing practices in NME psychiatric hospitals. NME retained Tomko to represent a former NME regional administrator, Cronen, but not NME.

While representing Cronen, Tomko moved to Baker & Botts. NME and Cronen had entered a joint-defense agreement and Tomko signed it. The agreement required the parties and their lawyers to keep certain information confidential. After Tomko joined Baker & Botts, he stopped representing Cronen. Several months later, other lawyers at the firm sued NME on behalf of former patients.

NME moved to disqualify Baker & Botts based on the joint-

---

[1] 924 S.W.2d 123 (Tex. 1996).

defense agreement. The Supreme Court concluded that Tomko's obligations under the agreement precluded him from undertaking representation adverse to NME, and that the resulting conflict was imputed to the law firm as well. The Court stated:

> Even though Tomko never represented NME, he was admitted into its confidences with his pledge to preserve them. . . . Tomko simply could not honor his obligations under the joint defense agreement and, at the same time, prosecute the pending claims against NME. Even if there were a way to do so, such conduct by an attorney would give a strong appearance of impropriety. . . . Tomko assumed that duty to NME expressly, and he could not honor it and sue NME at the same time. . . . [I]f Tomko had represented NME, Baker & Botts would be disqualified from representing plaintiffs suing NME, irrespective of the evidence and the district court's finding. The attorney's knowledge is imputed by law to every other attorney in the firm. There is, in effect, an irrebuttable presumption that an attorney in a law firm has access to the confidences of the clients and former clients of other attorneys in the firm. . . . We perceive no reason why the presumption should not apply. The attorney's duty to preserve confidences shared under a joint defense agreement is no less because the person to whom they belong was never a client. The attorney's promise places him in the role of a fiduciary, the same as toward a client.[2]

---

[2] *Id.* at 129, 130-31 (citations omitted). *See also Wilson P. Abraham Constr. Corp. v. Armco Steel Corp.*, 559 F.2d 250, 253 (5th Cir. 1977) (discussed in *Godbey*); ABA Comm. on Ethics and Prof. Resp., Formal Op. 95-395

A joint defense agreement or arrangement need not be in writing to require disqualification.[3] Rather, receiving confidential information from non-clients could itself require disqualification.[4]

(1997) (discussing the obligations of a lawyer who formerly represented a client in connection with a joint defense consortium); *cf. In re Mitcham,* 133 S.W.3d 274 (Tex. 2004) (concluding that when a plaintiffs' law firm hired a lawyer who previously had been a legal assistant for a law firm representing TXU in asbestos cases, and in the process of hiring the lawyer the new employer-firm negotiated a conflicts-avoidance agreement in which the new employer-firm agreed not to participate in any asbestos suit against TXU or share information about them, the firm was disqualified; and stating that "[b]because [the firm] cannot give the [plaintiffs] the representation to which they are entitled without mentioning facts surrounding TXU's use of asbestos (which [the] agreement precludes [the firm] from doing), [the firm is] disqualified").

[3] *See In re Skiles,* 102 S.W.3d 323, 326-27 (Tex. App.—Beaumont 2003, orig. proceeding) (granting mandamus relief to require disqualification, and holding that communications with a lawyer representing an insurer in a coverage suit concerning matters of common interest were sufficient to trigger later disqualification of his firm, even though no written joint-defense agreement existed and even though the movant-insured and the insurer were never co-defendants); *Rio Hondo Implement Co. v. Euresti,* 903 S.W.2d 128, 132-33 (Tex. App.—Corpus Christi 1995, orig. proceeding) ("holding that participation in a joint defense could be cause for counsel's disqualification.").

[4] *See In re Reynosa,* 361 S.W.3d 719, 724 (Tex. App.—Corpus Christi 2012, orig. proceeding) (disqualifying lawyer when a nonclient had shared information concerning claims for the "common cause" of resolving the nonclient's claims).

Chapter 10

Disqualification of Cocounsel

§ 10.1 Introduction.

When one lawyer is disqualified in a matter and is also working with cocounsel, the question arises whether cocounsel is disqualified. The Texas Supreme Court set out the controlling standards in *In re American Home Prods. Corp.*[1]

§ 10.2 The *American Home* standards.

American Home arose from litigation involving Norplant, the contraceptive implant. The Herrera and Harrison law firms were cocounsel for plaintiffs. Herrera hired a "freelance consultant," Palacios, who previously had served as a legal assistant for a law firm defending the manufacturer, Wyeth. The supreme court concluded that because Herrera failed to screen Palacios, Herrera and his law firm were disqualified under the *Grant* and *Phoenix Founders* principles applicable to nonlawyer-staff conflicts.[2] Then the court analyzed whether cocounsel, Harrison, was disqualified from either of the two possible sources, cocounsel Herrera or legal assistant Palacios.

The court first addressed the possible disqualification of Harrison based on Herrera. The court noted that while Herrera was "conclusively presumed" to possess Wyeth's confidential information, the record did not reflect that Palacios had actually disclosed Wyeth's confidential information to him. Consequently, the question was whether to re-impute Herrera's knowledge to Harrison. The court observed that other courts that had considered the issue of cocounsel re-imputation had focused on several factors, including "whether disqualified counsel actually possessed

---

[1] 985 S.W.2d 68 (Tex. 1998).

[2] *See* Chapter 13.

confidential information, the relationship between disqualified counsel and co-counsel, the role that both the tainted attorney and co-counsel have played in the underlying litigation, the likelihood that confidences have been shared, and the extent to which the tainted attorney has acted as a conduit of information to co-counsel."[3]

The court then established a two-step test for determining whether disqualification of cocounsel is necessary in these circumstances:

1. The party seeking disqualification first must demonstrate (a) that disqualified counsel and cocounsel had "substantive conversations" with one another, (b) that they engaged in "joint preparation for trial," or (c) that cocounsel apparently had received confidential information.[4] If the party seeking disqualification of cocounsel makes one of those showings, the presumption arises that cocounsel received the adversary's confidential information and the burden of showing non-disclosure shifts to the party opposing disqualification.

2. The party opposing disqualification then "may rebut this presumption by providing probative and material evidence that the tainted person, in this case Herrera, did not disclose confidential information of his adversary."[5]

---

[3] *Id.* at 79 (citations omitted).

[4] *Id.* at 81.

[5] *Id.*; *but see In re CMH Homes, Inc.*, 2013 WL 2446724, at *5 (Tex. App.—San Antonio, orig. proceeding.) (holding that disqualified counsel's previous legal representation of client on a substantially related matter created an irrebuttable presumption that counsel not only possessed confidential information but also shared confidential information with cocounsel, and interpreting the phrase "associated with" under Rule 1.09(b) "to include not only partners, employees, and associates within the same firm, but individuals working together on a case or issue regardless

The court recognized that the prescribed procedure might create a disadvantage for the party seeking disqualification to respond to the rebuttal evidence offered by the party opposing disqualification. Attorney-client, work-product, and other privileges might make it difficult to obtain the evidence necessary to contest the rebuttal evidence. While the party seeking disqualification should not be "permitted to broadly pierce privileges to probe" whether actual disclosure of confidential information had occurred, the party should be entitled to determine whether co-counsel had jointly prepared the case for trial or had had substantive discussion concerning the case, without inquiring into "the substance of the work . . . done or of discussions between co-counsel."[6]

The court also recognized that even if the party opposing disqualification successfully rebutted the presumption of disclosure of confidential information initially, later developments in the case might allow the party seeking disqualification to reurge the motion to disqualify. For example, during further discovery or even at trial, circumstances might make it appear that cocounsel was using the adversary's confidential information. In that situation, disqualification would be appropriate if "the only source of information sought to be used by co-counsel was an improper conduit."[7]

Concerning cocounsel Harrison's possible disqualification, the court first noted the irrebuttable presumption that Palacios possessed Wyeth's confidential information and that by failing to screen her, Herrera had failed to rebut the presumption that she had shared the confidential information with him. If Herrera had properly screened her, that also would have protected his cocounsel.

---

of their actual status as a member of the firm, of-counsel, or *co-counsel*. To hold to the contrary, that Rule 1.09(b) only applies to actual employees of the same law firm, would amount to disregarding the plain and common meaning of 'associate with.'") (emphasis added).

[6] *Id.*

[7] *Id.* at 81-82.

However, the court concluded, Herrera's failure to screen Palacios did not automatically disqualify cocounsel. Instead, the issue of cocounsel disqualification turned on "the nature of the contact and communications between co-counsel and the nonlawyer . . . ."[8] Disqualification would be necessary (1) if the nonlawyer had disclosed confidential information to cocounsel, or (2) if the nonlawyer and cocounsel had "worked so closely together or the nature of their communications was such that there is a substantial likelihood that confidential information was shared."[9] Again, the court established a two-step process:

1. The party seeking disqualification first must establish that contact or communication occurred between the tainted nonlawyer and cocounsel.

2. Then the burden shifts to the party opposing disqualification of cocounsel to show (a) that "there was no reasonable prospect that the opposing party's confidential information was disclosed," *and* (b) that no confidential information was disclosed.

A substantial threat of disclosure would exist, the court concluded, if the nonlawyer and cocounsel worked together on a matter from which the nonlawyer should have been screened and the nonlawyer substantively communicated with cocounsel concerning the matter.[10]

---

[8] *Id.* at 77.

[9] *Id.*

[10] *Id.* at 78.

But the court also identified three circumstances in which disqualification would not be appropriate:

1. The only contact between the nonlawyer and cocounsel consisted of "casual greetings or similar passing contact," and cocounsel "did not review or otherwise become aware of" the nonlawyer's work product.

2. The nonlawyer and cocounsel had some other contact or communications, or cocounsel was otherwise privy to the nonlawyer's work product, but the contact, communications, and work product did not relate to matters in which the nonlawyer should have been screened.

3. Communications did occur concerning the matter in which the nonlawyer should have been screened, but the communications were solely from the lawyer to the nonlawyer.[11]

---

[11] *Id.*

Chapter 11

Disqualification of Successor Counsel

§ 11.1 Introduction. In *In re George*,[1] the Texas Supreme Court addressed the proper procedures for disqualified counsel to transfer a client's file to successor counsel without tainting and potentially disqualifying successor counsel. The court also explained the steps for the trial court to follow in overseeing the transfer process.

§ 11.2 *In re George* Standards. The facts in *George* began with *In re EPIC Holdings, Inc.*,[2] in which the supreme court disqualified two law firms that represented a plaintiff. The plaintiff was an employee who sued to challenge a merger that involved a corporation owned in part by an employee stock ownership plan. The supreme court disqualified the employee's counsel based upon counsel's prior affiliation with the law firm involved in forming the corporation.

After the *EPIC Holdings* decision, the parties that had moved for disqualification of those firms then objected to the transfer of the work product of the disqualified lawyers to the new lawyers. That led to the decision in *George*.

The supreme court in *George* identified two categories of documents that might be in issue when disqualified counsel transfers the client file to successor counsel. The first category consists of documents in the public record or exchanged by the parties—including pleadings, discovery, and correspondence. The supreme court held that successor counsel is "presumptively entitled" to receive those documents. However, the court recognized that even for that category, "the possibility exists" that the disqualified lawyer could reveal confidential

---

[1] 28 S.W.3d 511 (Tex. 2000).

[2] 985 S.W.2d 41 (Tex. 1998).

information in those documents.

The second category is work product. The court held that a rebuttable presumption exists that the work product contains the former client's confidential information. The current client may rebut that presumption by demonstrating that a "substantial likelihood" does not exist that particular items contain the former client's confidential information.

The supreme court identified these steps for the trial court to take if the former client moves to restrict access to work product or if successor counsel moves to obtain access to the documents:

1. Preparation of inventory. The trial court should order the disqualified lawyers to produce a work-product inventory. The inventory should describe "the type of work, the subject matter of the item, the claims it relates to and any other factor the court considers relevant."[3] If an item of work product covers more than one claim or subject, the inventory should indicate that fact. The trial court also should consider the nature and subject matter of the work product. "For example, deposition or case summaries are less likely to contain confidential information than a disqualified attorney's notes. . . . Legal research on certain procedural or evidentiary issues is unlikely to be tainted."[4]

2. Trial court analysis of uncertain items. If the trial court is unable to determine from the inventory whether a particular item is tainted, the trial court should consider "any other evidence" presented by successor counsel. For "questionable items,"

---

[3] *George*, 28 S.W.3d at 518.

[4] *Id.* at 519.

the court may conduct an in camera inspection. Finally, if the trial court remains unsure whether an item is tainted, "then the presumption is not rebutted and the material cannot be turned over to successor counsel."[5]

---

[5] *Id.*

Chapter 12

Disqualification for Receipt of Privileged Information

§ 12.1 Introduction. A lawyer who improperly receives or reviews privileged or confidential information of an opposing party may be subject to disqualification. The two leading Texas Supreme Court decisions are *In re Meador*[1] and *In re Nitla S.A. de C.V.*[2] In *Meador* the supreme court set out the basic standards governing disqualification when a lawyer receives privileged information outside the normal discovery process. In *Nitla* the court addressed an unusual situation in which the trial judge required one party to deliver privileged documents to the opposing party, and then, after the lawyer had already reviewed the privileged documents, the court of appeals reversed the trial court's determination.

§ 12.2 *In re Meador.*

In *Meador*,[3] a lawyer represented plaintiff Meador in an employment case against Meador's former employer, CLN. Meador alleged, among other things, that CLN's former general manager, Dowdle, had sexually harassed her. When Meador sued CLN, CLN already had its own suit pending against Dowdle for fraud. The CLN-Dowdle case later settled. At the time, a current CLN employee, Peterson, worked for CLN's president, Nichols, and had access to his documents and mail. Peterson saw a letter from CLN's lawyers concerning the settlement and mentioning a statement that Dowdle had agreed to give in Meador's case. Peterson copied the documents and also copied a chronology of events that CLN's lawyers prepared concerning Meador's case. She later saw and read the

---

[1] 968 S.W.2d 346 (Tex. 1998).

[2] 92 S.W.3d 419 (Tex. 2002).

[3] 968 S.W.2d 346 (Tex. 1998).

statement that Dowdle gave as a part of the settlement.[4]

Later, Peterson decided to pursue her own claim against CLN. She took the documents she had copied to Meador's lawyer, Masterson, and retained him. He produced the documents in Meador's case, and CLN then filed a motion to disqualify him. The trial judge denied the motion.[5]

The Texas Supreme Court recognized that no rule specifically addresses this particular situation: a lawyer who does not personally engage in wrongdoing receives an opposing party's privileged materials without authorization and outside the formal pretrial discovery process. Nonetheless, the court concluded, a court has the power "under appropriate circumstances" to disqualify a lawyer even if the lawyer has not violated a specific disciplinary rule.[6] A lawyer who uses improperly obtained privileged materials "potentially subverts the litigation process."[7] But no "bright-line standard" applies to the disqualification proceeding, and the inquiry is fact-intensive.[8]

The court of appeals in *Meador* had concluded that disqualification was necessary. The court of appeals had relied on the guidelines set out in ABA Formal Opinion 94-382:

> A lawyer who receives on an unauthorized basis materials of an adverse party that she knows to be privileged or confidential should, upon recognizing the privileged or confidential nature of the materials, either refrain from reviewing such materials or review them only to the extent required to determine how appropriately to proceed; she should notify her

---

[4] *Id.* at 348.

[5] *Id.* at 349.

[6] *Id.* at 351.

[7] *Id.*

[8] *Id.*

adversary's lawyer that she has such materials and should either follow instructions of the adversary's lawyer with respect to the disposition of the materials, or refrain from using the materials until a definitive resolution of the proper disposition of the materials is obtained from a court.

The supreme court concluded that while lawyers should "aspire" to that standard in dealing with an opponent's privileged materials, that was not the proper standard for disqualification.[9]

Instead, the supreme court set out a non-exclusive list of factors for a trial court to consider in determining disqualification in light of the relevant facts:

In sum, the trial court, giving due consideration to the importance of our discovery privileges, must consider all the facts and circumstances to determine whether the interests of justice require disqualification. In this exercise of judicial discretion, a trial court should consider, among others, these factors:

1) whether the attorney knew or should have known that the material was privileged;

2) the promptness with which the attorney notifies the opposing side that he or she has received its privileged information;

3) the extent to which the attorney reviews and

---

[9] *Id.* In 2002, the ABA added Model Rule 4.4(b). That Rule provides that when a lawyer receives a document that the lawyer "knows or reasonably should know that the document was inadvertently sent," the lawyer shall "promptly notify the sender." The ABA Committee then issued Formal Opinion 06-440, withdrawing Opinion 94-382.

digests the privileged information;

4) the significance of the privileged information; i.e., the extent to which its disclosure may prejudice the movant's claim or defense, and the extent to which return of the documents will mitigate that prejudice;

5) the extent to which movant may be at fault for the unauthorized disclosure;

6) the extent to which the nonmovant will suffer prejudice from the disqualification of his or her attorney.[10]

The court emphasized that those factors apply only when a lawyer receives privileged materials outside the normal discovery process, and the lawyer was not involved in wrongfully procuring an opponent's privileged documents.[11]

Based upon the record, the supreme court concluded that while some of the factors cut in favor of disqualification, others did not. The court identified these factors as favoring disqualification:

- Masterson should have known "after the most cursory review" that the materials were privileged.

---

[10] *Id.* at 351-52.

[11] *Id.* at 352. As stated by the court, "[i]f a lawyer receives privileged materials because the opponent inadvertently produced them in discovery, the lawyer ordinarily has no duty to notify the opponent or voluntarily return the materials." *Id. See also In re Parnham*, 263 S.W.3d 97, 103-106 (Tex. App.—Houston [1st Dist.] 2006, orig. proceeding) (holding that when Parnham's lawyer reviewed and tried to copy privileged documents that had been inadvertently produced during discovery, neither *Meador* nor *Nitla* applied; instead, the snap-back provision of Tex. R. Civ. P. 193.3 controlled, allowing the party that produced the documents to recover them, but not authorizing disqualification).

- Masterson did not notify CLN when he received the documents, though his clients did produce the documents at their depositions.

- Masterson "thoroughly reviewed" the materials.

- Masterson specifically referred to portions of the documents in responding to CLN's motion for sanctions.

- CLN was not at fault, because Peterson had secretly copied and taken the documents.[12]

But the court concluded that these factors supported the trial court's ruling and militated against disqualification:

- The information did not appear to "significantly prejudice" CLN in the Meador suit.

- The settlement letter did not set out the contents of the statement that Dowdle had agreed to give, and Peterson had not taken the statement with her when she left CLN.

- Most of the remaining documents were CLN's president's handwritten notes from mediation and from meetings with CLN's lawyers, but CLN did not identify anything in the notes that would be likely to significantly prejudice CLN.

- Meador would suffer "serious hardship" if the court disqualified Masterson because he was both handling her claims and defending her against CLN counterclaims of over $1 million for malpractice in her services as a financial consultant.

---

[12] *In re Meador,* 968 S.W.2d 346, 352 (Tex. 1998).

On balance, the supreme court held that the trial court did not abuse its discretion in not disqualifying Masterson.[13]

§ 12.3 *In re Nitla.*

In *In re Nitla*,[14] at the conclusion of a discovery hearing, the trial judge gave privileged materials directly to a lawyer, but then the court of appeals reversed the trial judge's ruling on the privilege issue. Specifically, the trial judge had ruled that Bank of America's documents in issue were not privileged, and then also denied Bank of America's request for an emergency stay of the ruling and simply handed the documents to Nitla's lawyer. After the court of appeals reversed the privilege ruling, Bank of America sought to disqualify Nitla's lawyer. In that unusual setting, the supreme court held that the *Meador* standards were inapplicable because they apply only "when a lawyer receives an opponent's privileged materials *outside the normal course of discovery*."[15] Instead, "when a party receives documents from a trial court, and a reviewing court later deems the documents privileged, the party moving to disqualify opposing counsel must show that: (1) opposing counsel's reviewing the privileged documents caused actual harm to the moving party; and (2) disqualification is necessary, because the trial court lacks any lesser means to remedy the moving party's harm."[16] The supreme court held that Bank of America could not make either showing: the documents merely allowed Nitla's counsel to identify four new witnesses to depose, and the trial court could use a less disruptive remedy, such as quashing the depositions.[17]

---

[13] *Id.* at 353. *See also In re Marketing Investors Corp.*, 80 S.W.3d 44, 51 (Tex. App.—Dallas 1998, orig. proceeding) (applying the *Meador* factors to disqualify lawyer who refused to return privileged documents that the client obtained after the employer terminated the client).

[14] *In re Nitla S.A. de C.V.*, 92 S.W.3d 419 (Tex. 2002).

[15] *Id.* at 423 (quoting *Meador*).

[16] *Id.*

[17] *Id.*

§ 12.4 *In re RSR Corp.*

Recently, the Texas Supreme Court reaffirmed the *Meador* factors and held that the *Meador* analysis applies when a fact witness discloses his past employer's privileged and confidential information to opposing counsel outside of the normal discovery process.

In *In re RSR Corp.*,[18] Bickel & Brewer represented RSR in a breach of contract case against a Chilean company, Inppamet. During the litigation, Inppamet's former finance manager, Sobarzo, met repeatedly with Bickel & Brewer and RSR's Chilean counsel, BMAJ. BMAJ hired Sobarzo as a paid consultant. In exchange, Sobarzo supplied the two law firms with significant information regarding Inppamet and the contested contract, including a pen drive with documents that Sobarzo had taken from his former employer.[19]

Inppamet moved to disqualify Bickel & Brewer. Relying on *In re American Home Products Corp.*, the trial court granted the motion and found that Bickel & Brewer should have treated Sobarzo as a side-switching paralegal and screened him from the case.[20]

The Supreme Court held that the standard in *American Home Products* was inapplicable. Instead, the *Meador* standard controlled in this setting involving a fact witness with confidential information of his former employer, when the employee's position with the employer existed independently of litigation and he did not primarily report to lawyers.[21]

The Court rejected Inppamet's argument that because Sobarzo became a paid consultant in the litigation, he was subject to screening that applies to a side-switching paralegal and that therefore the *American Home Products* disqualification analysis controlled. The

---

[18] 2015 WL 7792871 (Tex. 2015).

[19] *Id.* at *2.

[20] *Id.* at *1-2.

[21] *Id.* at *3-4.

Court held that the *American Home Products* standard applies only to "paralegals, legal assistants, or other nonlawyers who are directly supervised by attorneys and are retained to assist with litigation."[22]

Chapter 13

Disqualifications Resulting From Nonlawyer Staff

§ 13.1 Introduction.

The same "migratory foul" problems that result in disqualifications of lawyers and law firms generally apply to nonlawyers—with one important exception: Texas decisions allow advance screening of nonlawyers to avoid disqualification.

§ 13.2 Nonlawyer staff disqualifications: in general.

Concurrent-conflict and former-client-conflict issues can arise when a law firm hires a nonlawyer. The problems occur most often when a legal assistant who works for a law firm that is on one side of a case switches employment to work for a law firm on the other side of the case. The issues can arise with almost any type of nonlawyer staff, including legal secretaries, investigators, law clerks, as well as with use of outsourced legal services. Similar issues can arise with in-house counsel or expert witnesses.

A proper pre-employment check to identify and address possible conflicts in advance is the key to avoiding these problems. Unfortunately, that doesn't always happen.

Texas courts generally allow screening of nonlawyers, but not screening of lawyers.[1] Courts have identified three justifications for the different treatment of nonlawyers: (1) Courts and lawyers should not "unduly restrict" the employment mobility of nonlawyers. (2) In some instances, nonlawyers may not have the same understanding of a client's confidential information or comparable ability to exploit that

---

[1] *See* Chapter 16.

information. Thus, the risk of harm may be less than from a tainted lawyer. (3) Nonlawyers typically do not have the same level of financial interest in the case as lawyers do.[2]

Nonetheless, if "a serious conflict of interest is present because of a nonlawyer's work on a matter that the nonlawyer previously worked on for opposing counsel, important public policies may balance in favor of disqualification."[3]

---

[2] *See In re Columbia Valley Healthcare Syst., L.P.*, 320 S.W.3d 819, 825-26 (Tex. 2010) ("We have stated that, as compared to lawyers, there is greater concern that the mobility of nonlawyers could be 'unduly restricted.' . . . Further, a nonlawyer employee may not have the same financial interest in the results of a case, nor the same understanding of confidential information as a lawyer." (citations omitted)).

[3] *Id.* at 826; *see also In re American Home Prods. Corp.*, 985 SW.2d 68, 76 (Tex. 1998) (disqualifying a law firm that failed to rebut the presumption that a nonlawyer shared confidential information with the new firm); *Phoenix Founders, Inc. v. Marshall*, 887 S.W.2d 831, 836 (Tex. 1994) (remanding for the trial court to determine whether the law firm had effectively screened the nonlawyer); *Grant v. Thirteenth Court of Appeals*, 888 S.W.2d 466, 468 (Tex. 1994) (requiring disqualification because of ineffective screening); (upholding disqualification when a firm did not effectively screen a nonlawyer who had been a member of the opposing party's litigation team, then hired, paid, and received information from the nonlawyer); *In re SAExploration, Inc.*, 2012 WL 6017717, at *4 (Tex. App.—Houston [14th Dist.] 2012, orig. proceeding) (upholding disqualification of an in-house counsel because of lack of effective screening; applying the nonlawyer-disqualification standards because the in-house counsel was not acting as a lawyer on the matter, but rather as a corporate officer); *In re Barnes*, 2003 WL 1848763, *1 (Tex. App.— Beaumont 2003, orig. proceeding) (concluding that the screening was effective); *but cf. In re Guaranty Ins. Servs., Inc.*, 343 S.W.3d 130, 136-37 (Tex. 2011) (disqualification not required even though the screening failed, despite the second firm's "exemplary" efforts, because the nonlawyer did not disclose confidential information, the second firm had "taken measures to reduce the potential for misuse of confidences to an acceptable level," and no evidence showed that the supervising lawyer "reasonably should have known about the conflict"); *Rubin v. Enns*, 23 S.W.3d 382, 388-89 (Tex. App.—Amarillo 2000, orig. proceeding [mand. denied]) (concluding that the screening was effective).

Thus, nonlawyers are subject to only the first of the two "conclusive," irrebuttable presumptions that normally apply to lawyers who have worked on a matter and then switch to another firm that is on the opposite side of the same matter or a substantially related matter: (1) at the first firm, the lawyer (or nonlawyer) *received* confidential information; (2) at the second firm, the lawyer (or nonlawyer) *shared* the confidential information. For nonlawyers, "effective screening" can rebut the second presumption concerning the possible sharing of confidential information at the new firm.

§ 13.3 Nonlawyer Disqualification Decisions: Texas Supreme Court.

The Texas Supreme Court has issued several decisions concerning nonlawyer disqualification.

In *Phoenix Founders, Inc. v. Marshall*,[4] a legal assistant had worked for the opposing counsel for only three weeks and had billed only 0.6 of an hour on the case in question. The supreme court remanded the case to determine if the law firm could show that it had "effectively screened the paralegal from any contact with the underlying suit." The supreme court held that the first conclusive presumption applied—that is, while at the opposing law firm, the legal assistant had received confidential information. But the second presumption—that the legal assistant had shared the information with the second law firm—was rebuttable by proper pre-hiring screening. The supreme court held that the screening should include cautioning the legal assistant "not to disclose any information relating to the representation of a client of the former employer" and not to "work on any matter on which the paralegal worked during the prior employment, or regarding which the paralegal has information relating to the former employer's representation." The firm also should take "other reasonable steps to ensure that the paralegal does not work in connection with matters on which

---

[4] 887 S.W.2d 831 (Tex. 1994).

the paralegal worked during the prior employment, absent client consent after consultation."[5]

Disqualification would be necessary if "information relating to the representation of an adverse client has in fact been disclosed" or if "screening would be ineffective or the nonlawyer necessarily would be required to work on the other side of a matter that is the same as or substantially related to a matter on which the nonlawyer has previously worked."[6]

The supreme court set out the factors for the lower court to consider on remand to determine the effectiveness of any screening:

> the substantiality of the relationship between the former and current matters; the time elapsing between the matters; the size of the firm; the number of individuals presumed to have confidential information; the nature of their involvement in the former matter; and the timing and features of any measures taken to reduce the danger of disclosure.[7]

In *Grant v. Thirteenth Court of Appeals*,[8] the supreme court applied the *Phoenix* standards to uphold a trial court's disqualification of a defense law firm that hired a legal secretary who had previously been the plaintiffs' lawyer's "primary coordinator" for the cases. At the plaintiffs' firm, the legal assistant had interviewed clients daily, opened files, prepared reports, and scheduled medical appointments. Although the defense firm had asked its temporary-service agency to inquire about possible conflicts, the firm had not asked the secretary

---

[5] *Id.* at 835.

[6] *Id.*

[7] *Id.* at 836.

[8] 888 S.W.2d 466 (Tex. 1994).

directly about possible conflicts. The supreme court held that the testimony of members of the defense firm that the secretary had not disclosed confidential information was inadequate to rebut the information-sharing presumption:

> The test for disqualification is met by demonstrating a genuine *threat* of disclosure, not an actual materialized disclosure. This rule encourages institutional measures to guard against any disclosure, whether deliberate or inadvertent. Moreover, any rule focusing on actual disclosure would place a virtually insurmountable burden on the party seeking disqualification, since the only persons who know whether confidences were actually shared will generally be the very lawyers seeking to avoid disqualification.[9]

The supreme court observed that the defense firm had allowed the secretary to work on "the very litigation that she had previously worked on for opposing counsel—even after the firm became aware that she had previously worked on the case."[10]

The supreme court elaborated on the required screening procedures in *In re Columbia Valley Healthcare Syst., L.P.*,[11] in which the court again upheld disqualification. The legal assistant in question had first worked for a law firm that was defending Columbia Valley in a medical malpractice case, and then worked for the firm that represented the plaintiffs in the same case. Although the plaintiffs' counsel had orally instructed the legal assistant not to work on that case or any other case that she had worked on at the defense firm,

---

[9] *Id.* at 467 (citations omitted).

[10] *Id.*

[11] 320 S.W.3d 819 (Tex. 2010).

she did so. [12]

The supreme court reiterated the *Phoenix* factors for determining whether a law firm's screening of a nonlawyer is effective, and concluded that while the firm had properly instructed the legal assistant not to work on any matter that she worked on during her prior employment, the firm had not met the "other reasonable measures" requirement. Specifically, "the other reasonable measures must include, at a minimum, formal, institutionalized screening measures that render the possibility of the nonlawyer having contact with the file less likely."[13]

In *In re Guaranty Insurance Services, Inc.*,[14] the supreme court addressed a nonlawyer screen that failed, but the court nonetheless concluded that disqualification was improper. The firm had taken several steps to avoid a conflict, including running the paralegal through a normal conflicts search before hiring him; instructing him several times not to disclose confidential information that he obtained in his previous employment; having him sign a confidentiality agreement and employee handbook with the same instructions; and directing him to notify his supervising attorney immediately if he became aware of a matter on which he previously worked. However, the paralegal forgot that at the prior law firm he had worked on and billed 6.8 hours on the same lawsuit that he was working on at his current firm. When the opposing counsel notified the firm of the conflict, the firm immediately instructed the paralegal to stop working on the case and not disclose any information from his prior employment. The evidence at the disqualification hearing showed that the paralegal had not disclosed any confidences from his earlier work.[15]

The supreme court concluded that whether screening works

---

[12] *Id.* at 822-23.

[13] *Id.* at 826.

[14] 343 S.W.3d 130 (Tex. 2011).

[15] *Id.* at 132-33.

effectively "is not determinative." Instead, quoting *Phoenix*, the court stated that the "ultimate question" is whether the second firm "has taken measures sufficient to *reduce* the potential for misuse of confidences to an *acceptable* level."[16] Here, even though the nonlawyer had worked on the same case at both law firms, no evidence showed that the supervising lawyer reasonably should have known of the conflict. The supreme court stated: "The failure of a screening method to actually screen a tainted party will not translate into disqualification where 'the practical effect of formal screening has been achieved.' . . . That effect was achieved here because there is no evidence the supervising attorney reasonably should have known about the conflict."[17]

In *In re RSR Corp.*,[18] the Texas Supreme Court made clear that the *Meador* standards apply when a former employee is retained as a paid consultant and provides counsel with confidential information of the former employer. The trial court had disqualified the plaintiffs' counsel because the firm had "worked so closely" with the defendant's former finance manager, Sobarzo. Relying on *In re American Home Products Corp.,* the trial judge treated the former employee as a side-switching paralegal and found that the law firm should have screened him from the case. The Supreme Court rejected that approach. The Court held that screening is not required for fact witnesses such as Sobarzo:

> His position with his former employer existed independently of litigation, and his function was not primarily to report to lawyers. Sobarzo was Inppamet's finance manager with firsthand knowledge of facts, and thus his contact with Inppamet lawyers, without more, does not shield him from RSR's contact. Indeed, we have only applied the *American Home Products* presumptions

---

[16] *Id.* at 134-35 (citations omitted; court's emphasis).

[17] *Id.* at 136.

[18] 2015 WL 7792871 (Tex. 2015).

to paralegals, legal assistants, or other nonlawyers who are directly supervised by attorneys and are retained to assist with litigation.[19]

Instead, the Court concluded that the factors in *In re Meador*[20] properly balanced Inppamet's need to protect privileged information against RSR's interest in retaining counsel.[21]

§ 13.4 Nonlawyer Disqualification Decisions: Courts of Appeals.

Texas courts of appeals have generally followed the nonlawyer-disqualification standards set by the Texas Supreme Court in *Phoenix* and its progeny. Some of those decisions have involved close analysis of the screening systems and others have addressed novel fact settings, such as in-house counsel and consulting experts. See, for example:

In re SAExploration, Inc.[22] — disqualifying an in-house counsel but applying the nonlawyer screening standards because of his multiple roles in the corporation: "Although Whiteley is an attorney, he is not participating in this case as retained, outside counsel. Whiteley wears multiple corporate hats as SAE's general counsel, chief operating officer, and chief financial officer."

---

[19] *Id.* at *5.

[20] 968 S.W.2d 346 (Tex. 1998) (orig. proceeding). *See* Chapter 12, above.

[21] In *RSR*, the Supreme Court disapproved of *In re Bell Helicopter Textron, Inc.*, 87 S.W.3d 139 (Tex. App.—Fort Worth 2002, orig. proceeding). Bell Helicopter applied the nonlawyer-disqualification standards from American Home Products to disqualify a consulting expert who was not hired for litigation purposes and was not directly supervised by lawyers. The Supreme Court held that the In re Meador standard applied, rather than the American Home Products standard. See In re RSR Corp., 2015 WL 7792871, at *6.

[22] 2012 WL 6017717, *4 (Tex. App.—Houston [14th Dist.] 2012, no pet.).

In re Bell Helicopter Textron, Inc.[23] — applying the nonlawyer screening standards to disqualify a consulting expert who was a former employee of Bell and had worked on cases involving the same model helicopter.

In re Barnes[24] — denying mandamus relief to overturn a trial court order refusing to disqualify counsel, and noting that the trial judge had conducted a hearing in which "counsel for the real parties in interest demonstrated the precautions implemented by counsel to effectively screen from the relators' cases the newly-hired legal secretary formerly employed by counsel for the relators."

Rubin vs. Enns[25] — concluding that the firm's screening system for a legal assistant was adequate to avoid disqualification, when the screening included: sending a memo to all lawyers and staff identifying the two cases concerning which the legal assistant might have confidential information; instructing the recipients that the legal assistant could not disclose any information concerning the cases, and that violations of the instructions would be grounds for termination; prohibiting the legal assistant from performing any work on the two cases or discussing either case or disclosing any information concerning the cases; prohibiting any lawyer or staff member from discussing the cases with the legal assistant or in her presence or giving her access to any of the documents or files in those cases; directing the removal of all computer information concerning

---

[23] 87 S.W.3d 139, 145-46 (Tex. App.—Fort Worth 2002, orig. proceeding [mand. denied]) disapproved of by *In re RSR Corp.*, 2015 WL 7792871 (Tex. 2015). In *RSR*, the Supreme Court disapproved of *Bell Helicopter* for applying the nonlawyer-disqualification standards from American Home Products to disqualify a consulting expert when the former employer had not hired the employee for litigation purposes and the employee was not directly supervised by lawyers. The trial court should have applied the test from *In re Meador*, to address whether disqualification was necessary because of the employee provided the lawyers with confidential information. *See In re RSR Corp.*, 2015 WL 7792871, at *6..

[24] 2003 WL 1848763, *1 (Tex. App.—Beaumont 2003, orig. proceeding).

[25] 23 S.W.3d 382, 388-89 (Tex. App.—Amarillo 2000, orig. proceeding).

the cases from the firm computer system; requiring that the files for those cases be kept in a locked file in the managing partner's office; limiting access to those files and requiring the return of the files at the end of each business day; and having the managing partner meet with each employee of the firm to discuss the policies and obtain written agreement to comply with those policies.

See also Restatement § 123 cmt. f — for imputation purposes, treating law students as nonlawyer employees, unless special circumstances apply, but treating students who have finished law school but are awaiting admission to practice as lawyers.[26]

---

[26] *Cf.* Tex. Comm. on Prof'l Ethics, Op. 644 (2014) (addressing a conflict of interest that arose when a law clerk (X) worked on a case at one law firm (Firm A), and later when the law clerk became licensed to practice law, went to work for the law firm (Firm B) that was on the other side of the case; and concluding that Rule 1.09 would not require disqualification because X "was not a lawyer at Firm A and therefore did not personally represent" the party even though he had worked on the matter; but concluding that representation by Firm B "would violate Rule 1.06(b)(2) because the representation . . . would reasonably appear to be adversely limited by . . . X's responsibilities to his former employer Firm A and to [the now opposing party] and by . . . X's own interests in avoiding claims for misuse of confidential information previously entrusted to him"; that the conflict was nonconsentable under Rule 1.06(c)(1) because X could not "reasonably believe" that his representation of Firm B's client "would not be materially affected by" his obligations to Firm A and its client; and that under Rule 1.06(f), no other lawyer at Firm A could represent the client; and that screening would not avoid the imputed conflict).

Chapter 14

Disciplinary Rule 4.02

The Anti-Contact Rule

§ 14.1 Introduction.

Rule 4.02, the anti-contact rule, provides a basis for disqualification that does not involve a traditional conflict of interest. The Rule generally prohibits a lawyer from communicating with a person represented by counsel without consent from that counsel.

The purpose of Disciplinary Rule 4.02 is "to preserve the integrity of the client-lawyer relationship by protecting the represented party from the superior knowledge and skill of the opposing lawyer."[1]

Rule 4.02(a) sets out the central prohibition against communicating with represented persons, and Rule 4.02(b) similarly prohibits certain communications with retained experts. Rule 4.02(c) explains how the Rule applies to represented entities, private or government. Rule 4.02(d) provides an exception that allows lawyers to give second opinions to persons represented by counsel.

Generally the Rule does not prohibit a lawyer from communicating with a person represented by counsel in these circumstances:

- When the lawyer is *not* representing a client in

---

[1] *Vickery v. Comm'n for Lawyer Discipline,* 5 S.W.3d 241, 259 (Tex. App.—Houston [14th Dist.] 1999, pet. denied) (quoting *In re News Am. Publ'g, Inc.,* 974 S.W.2d 97, 100 (Tex. App.—San Antonio 1998, orig. proceeding) (en banc)); *see also* Rule 4.02 cmt. 1 (stating that the rule is "directed at efforts to circumvent the lawyer-client relationship").

making the communication.

- When the communication is *not* regarding the "subject of the representation."

- When the communication occurs when the lawyer does not know the person is represented by counsel.

- When the person's lawyer consents to the communication.

- When the communication is authorized by law (e.g., sending a statutorily required notice).[2]

Rule 4.02 also does not prohibit communications directly between clients as long as the lawyer does not "cause or encourage" the communication.[3]

§ 14.2 Communications with Represented Persons.

Rule 4.02(a) sets out the basic anti-contact prohibition against communicating with represented persons:

> (a) In representing a client, a lawyer shall not communicate or cause or encourage another to communicate about the subject of the

---

[2] See *Lee v. Fenwick*, 907 S.W.2d 88, 89-90 (Tex. App.—Eastland 1995, writ denied) (holding that a communication directly with an opposing party to give notice of a claim to comply with a prejudgment interest statute would not violate Rule 4.02, which allows such communications when "authorized by law"); Tex. Comm. on Prof'l Ethics, Op. 492 (1994) (addressing issues concerning a staff lawyer employed by a "labor organization" that provided assistance for city employees in presenting grievances and in nonjudicial resolution of workplace problems, and concluding that the pertinent state statute governing public employee grievances allowed communications with city employees involved in that procedure).

[3] *See* Rule 4.02 cmt. 2; ABA Formal Op. 11-461 (2011) (addressing what a lawyer may tell a client concerning direct client-to-client communications, under Model Rule 4.2).

> representation with a person, organization or entity of government the lawyer knows to be represented by another lawyer regarding that subject, unless the lawyer has the consent of the other lawyer or is authorized by law to do so.

A lawyer who violates that prohibition is subject to disqualification or other sanctions.[4]

The prohibition applies when these conditions are met:

- The communicating lawyer is "representing a client."

- The communication concerns the "subject of the representation."

- The communicating lawyer "knows" that another lawyer represents the person regarding the subject of the communication.

The two key exceptions that allow a lawyer to communicate with a represented person are: (1) the consent of opposing counsel; (2) a law authorizing the communication.

In *In re Users Systems, Inc.,*[5] the Texas Supreme Court addressed the question of when a lawyer "knows" that a person is represented by counsel. The supreme court upheld the trial court's decision not to disqualify lawyers who met with an opposing party. The meeting occurred at the opposing party's request and after that party informed the lawyers that he was no longer represented by counsel; however, the party's lawyers

---

[4] *See, e.g., Shelton v. Hess*, 599 F. Supp. 905, 910-11 (S.D. Tex. 1984) (disqualifying a plaintiff's lawyer who met several times with the defendant without the defense counsel's knowledge or consent); *see also* § 14.6, below.

[5] 22 S.W.3d 331 (Tex. 1999).

had not yet formally withdrawn from representation.[6] The court noted that ABA Formal Opinion 95-396 had concluded that "the communicating lawyer should not proceed without reasonable assurance that the representation has in fact been terminated," but the court held that while that procedure might be a "sensible course" of action in many instances, "that does not make it a prerequisite to communication in every instance under Rule 4.02." The court stated that "Rule 4.02 forbids a lawyer from communicating with another person only if the lawyer *knows* the person has legal counsel in the matter."[7]

§ 14.3 Communication with Retained Experts.

Rule 4.02(b) similarly prohibits communicating with an opponent's expert witness, without the consent of opposing counsel:

> (b) In representing a client a lawyer shall not communicate or cause another to communicate about the subject of representation with a person or organization a lawyer knows to be employed or retained for the purpose of conferring with or advising another lawyer about the subject of the representation, unless the lawyer has the consent of the other lawyer or is authorized by law to do so.

---

[6] *Id.* at 332-33.

[7] *Id.* at 334. *See also* Tex. Disciplinary R. Professional Conduct, Preamble: Terminology ("'Knows' denotes actual knowledge of the fact in question. A person's knowledge may be inferred from circumstances."); Restatement § 99 cmt. n (stating that a court may order disqualification "when necessary to protect against a significant risk of future misuse of confidential information obtained through the contact, when the contact has substantially interfered with the client's relationship with the client's lawyer, or when disqualification is appropriate to deter flagrant or reckless violations").

While the expert-contact prohibition occasionally results in disqualification or evidence exclusion,[8] the Rule can pose analytical challenges with multi-purpose experts—e.g., experts who simultaneously occupy the roles of treating physician, fact witness, and retained expert.

§ 14.4 Employees of Opposing Entity-Party.

Rule 4.02(c) explains how the rule applies to entities—private or government:

> (c) For the purpose of this rule, "organization or entity of government" includes: (1) those persons presently having a managerial responsibility with an organization or entity of government that relates to the subject of the representation, or (2) those persons presently employed by such organization or entity and whose act or omission in connection with the subject of representation may make

---

[8] *Cf. Cramer v. Sabine Transp. Co.*, 141 F. Supp.2d 727, 732-33 (S.D. Tex. 2001) (holding that disqualification of defense counsel was not required based on a single communication with plaintiff's expert when it was unclear whether the communication was about the "subject of representation" and no evidence showed that defense counsel initiated the meeting or encouraged the expert to relay confidential information); *Aguilar v. Morales*, 162 S.W.3d 825, 833 (Tex. App.—El Paso 2005, pet. denied) (concluding that a party violated Rule 4.02 by contacting a consulting expert, that the violation was discovery misconduct under Tex. R. Civ. P. 215, and that the trial court did not err in refusing to admit evidence from the improperly contacted expert; "The evidence reflects that Mr. Aguilar knew that Wicker did not want to reveal the identity of his consulting expert because he feared that Mr. Aguilar would contact Maly without his consent. After learning the consulting expert's identity, Mr. Aguilar proceeded to not only contact Maly without Wicker's consent but he actually hired Maly and Frontera Environmental to serve as the Aguilars' designated expert witnesses in the case. This effectively deprived Trujillo of his consulting experts. We conclude that Mr. Aguilar's contact with Maly constituted an abuse of the discovery process.").

the organization or entity of government vicariously liable for such act or omission.

For example, in *Hornsby v. Tarrant County College Dist.*,[9] the court disqualified plaintiff's counsel who improperly communicated with college employees who participated in the employment decision that was in issue.[10]

The Rule also does not prohibit a lawyer from contacting a *former* employee of an adverse entity-party.[11]

§ 14.5 Second Opinions.

Rule 4.02(d) has an exception that allows lawyers to give second opinions to persons who are represented by other lawyers:

(d) When a person, organization, or entity of

---

[9] 2013 WL 2093155 (Tex. App.—Fort Worth 2013, pet. denied).

[10] *Id.* at *6-7. *See also* Tex. Comm. on Prof'l Ethics, Op. 474 (1992) (holding that Rule 4.02 prohibited the lawyer for a plaintiff who had sued a city from calling a city council member to express disapproval of the city's settlement offer without obtaining permission of the city's lawyer); ABA Comm. on Ethics and Prof. Resp., Op. 97-408 (1997) (analyzing when, under Model Rule 4.2, a lawyer may contact a governmental entity, and concluding generally that "a lawyer representing a private party in a controversy with the government [may] communicate about the matter with government officials having authority to take or to recommend action in the matter, provided that the sole purpose of the communication is to address a policy issue, including settling the controversy," but that "[i]n such a situation the lawyer must give government counsel reasonable advance notice of his intent to communicate with such officials in order to afford them an opportunity to seek advice of counsel before deciding whether to entertain the communication").

[11] Rule 4.02 cmt. 4 ("[T]his Rule does not prohibit a lawyer from contacting a former employee of a represented organization or entity of a government, nor from contacting a person presently employed by such an organization or entity whose conduct is not a matter at issue but who might possess knowledge concerning the matter at issue.").

government that is represented by a lawyer in a matter seeks advice regarding that matter from another lawyer, the second lawyer is not prohibited by paragraph (a) from giving such advice without notifying or seeking consent of the first lawyer.

When a client who has a lawyer approaches another lawyer for a "second opinion," Rule 4.02(d) allows the second lawyer to consult with the client without seeking or obtaining consent from the first lawyer.[12]

§ 14.6 Other Remedies for Rule 4.02 Violations.

Disqualification is not the only remedy for a Rule 4.02 violation. For example, a court may suppress or exclude evidence that was obtained in violation of the anti-contact rule or may sanction a lawyer who violates the anti-contact prohibition.[13]

---

[12] *See* Rule 4.02 cmt. 2 (Rule 4.02 "does not prohibit a lawyer from furnishing a 'second opinion' in a matter to one requesting such opinion, nor from discussing employment in the matter if requested to do so"); *Upchurch v. Albear*, 5 S.W.3d 274, 279 (Tex. App.—Amarillo 1999, pet. denied) (noting that when a represented client approached a second lawyer to seek advice concerning a proposed settlement, Rule 4.02 did not prevent the second lawyer from advising the client regarding the settlement).

[13] *See, e.g., Aguilar v. Morales*, 162 S.W.3d 825, 833 (Tex. App.—El Paso 2005, pet. denied) (concluding that a party violated Rule 4.02 by contacting a consulting expert and that the violation was discovery misconduct under Tex. R. Civ. P. 215, and that the trial court did not err in refusing to admit evidence from the improperly contacted expert); *Richmond Condominiums v. Skipworth Commercial Plumbing, Inc.*, 245 S.W.3d 646, 660-61 (Tex. App.—Fort Worth 2008, pet. denied) (holding that trial court erred in failing to sanction defense counsel for violating Rule 4.02 by improperly contacting the joint venturers who were members of the plaintiff joint venture without permission of plaintiff's counsel in order to obtain affidavits that defendants were not at fault in fire damage suit; but holding that when no evidence showed that defendants were aware of or complicit in defense counsel's misconduct, reversal was inappropriate).

Chapter 15

Other Grounds For Disqualification

§ 15.1 Introduction.

The conflict-of-interest disciplinary rules are the most common grounds for disqualification motions. However, disqualification motions sometimes rely upon other disciplinary rules, statutes, regulations, or a court's inherent power to sanction.

§ 15.2 Other disciplinary rules.

As discussed above, the Texas Supreme Court has repeatedly emphasized that trial courts are to look to the Texas Disciplinary Rules of Professional Conduct for "guidance" in ruling on disqualification motions.[1] While disqualification motions most often rely on the conflict-of-interest rules, other disciplinary rules also sometimes provide grounds for disqualification. Two other disciplinary rules most frequently relied on are Rules 1.15 and 7.06.[2]

§ 15.3 Other disciplinary rules: Rule 1.15.

Rule 1.15 addresses withdrawal and termination of representation. In some circumstances, withdrawal is mandatory. Thus, a lawyer "shall decline to represent a client or, where representation has commenced, *shall withdraw*" from representation if:

> 1. The representation would violate Rule 3.08, the lawyer-as-witness rule.[3]

---

[1] *See* Chapter 3, above.

[2] *See also* Chapter 14, above (concerning disqualification under Rule 4.02, the anti-contact rule).

[3] Rule 1.15(a)(1). *See* Chapter 8, above.

2. The representation will result in violation of *any* "applicable rule[] of professional conduct."[4]

3. The representation will result in violation of any "other law."[5]

4. The lawyer's "physical, mental or psychological condition materially impairs the lawyer's fitness to represent the client."[6]

5. The lawyer is "discharged, with or without good cause."[7]

However, even in those situations, a lawyer must continue the representation if a court orders the lawyer to continue the representation.[8]

Thus, the general categories of mandatory withdrawal in Rule 1.15 embrace several factual settings. Consequently, when a party learns that a ground for mandatory withdrawal applies to opposing counsel, but opposing counsel is failing or refusing to withdraw, that circumstance may give rise to a motion to disqualify.[9]

---

[4] Rule 1.15(a)(1).

[5] *Id.*; *see, e.g., In re Texas Windstorm Ins. Assoc.*, 417 S.W.3d 119, 140 (Tex. App.—Houston [1st Dist.] 2013, orig. proceeding) (granting mandamus relief in a 2-1 decision and overturning disqualification of counsel, but noting that the trial judge had concluded that disqualified lawyers had violated the applicable TWIA conflict-of-interest regulation that imposed a five-year bar on representation, and had further concluded that the regulation qualified as a "law" under Rule 1.15(a)(1)).

[6] Rule 1.15(a)(2).

[7] Rule 1.15(a)(3). However, complications arise if the client becomes mentally incompetent. *See* Rule 1.15 cmt. 6.

[8] Rule 1.15(a), (c).

[9] In that situation, of course, ordinarily the party or lawyer who suspects that a basis for mandatory withdrawal applies to opposing counsel first should raise the issue informally or by written notice, rather than by filing a motion

§ 15.4 Other Disciplinary Rules: Rule 7.06.

Rule 7.06 generally prohibits a lawyer from accepting or continuing employment when the employment results from improper solicitation, barratry, or other illegal conduct.[10]

The prohibition in Rule 7.06(a) applies when the lawyer "knows or reasonably should know" that the employment was procured by conduct that violates these rules:

- Rules 7.01 through 7.05, which address solicitation and advertising.[11]

- Rule 8.04(a)(9), which prohibits barratry "as defined by the law of this state." The principal statute prohibiting barratrous conduct is § 38.12 of the Texas Penal Code.[12]

- Rule 8.04(a)(2), which prohibits a lawyer from committing a "serious crime" or "any other criminal act that reflects adversely on the lawyer's honesty, trustworthiness or fitness as a lawyer in other respects." Rule 8.04(b), in turn, defines "serious crime" to mean "barratry; any felony involving moral turpitude; any misdemeanor involving theft, embezzlement, or fraudulent misappropriation of

---

to disqualify. *Cf.* Texas Lawyer's Creed art. III.19 (stating that a lawyer is not to seek disqualification "unless it is necessary for the protection of my client's lawful objectives or is fully justified by the circumstances.").

[10] The Rule thus also triggers the mandatory withdrawal under Rule 1.15(a)(1) because continued representation would violate a "rule of professional conduct or other law."

[11] *See* Rules 7.01 (Firm Names and Letterhead), 7.02 (Communications Concerning A Lawyer's Services), 7.03 (Prohibited Solicitations and Payments), 7.04 (Advertisements in the Public Media), and 7.05 (Prohibited Written, Electronic, or Digital Solicitations).

[12] *See also* Tex. Gov't Code §§ 82.065-.0651 (setting out civil remedies for barratry for clients and nonclients).

money or other property, or any attempt, conspiracy, or solicitation of another" to commit any of those crimes. As a practical matter, in the context of Rule 7.06(a), Rule 8.04(a)(2) generally overlaps with the barratry prohibition in Rule 8.04(a)(9).

Rule 7.06(a) prohibits continuing the employment if the improper procurement was by the lawyer personally or by anyone else the lawyer "ordered, encouraged, or knowingly permitted" to engage in the conduct. Rule 7.06(b) extends the prohibition to the situation in which a lawyer "knows or reasonably should know" that another person in the firm (including of counsel) engaged in the conduct or ordered, encouraged, or permitted another to engage in the conduct.

Rule 7.06(c) sets out an exception to the prohibition on continuing employment when the lawyer has not personally violated paragraphs (a) or (b) of the Rule. The exception provides that if the lawyer accepts employment innocently but later comes to know, or reasonably should know, that the person who procured the lawyer's employment violated the specified rules, the lawyer may continue employment if "nothing of value is given thereafter for that employment."[13]

In litigation, defendants sometimes learn or suspect that a plaintiff's counsel may have obtained a case improperly in violation of those rules or statutes. That may lead to a motion to disqualify plaintiff's counsel. Obviously, a trial court should not entertain a defendant's proposed "fishing expedition"

---

[13] But note Rule 7.03(d) (providing that a lawyer shall not "charge for, or collect a fee for professional employment obtained in violation of Rule 7.03(a),(b), or (c)"). *See also* Tex. Gov't Code § 82.065(c) (providing for a quantum meruit recovery for a lawyer when the lawyer's contract is voided because of specified barratrous conduct, but the client does not show that the lawyer engaged in the conduct or knew about it in advance, and if the lawyer reports the misconduct or if one of two exceptions to the reporting requirement applies).

that focuses on the mere possibility that a plaintiff's counsel improperly solicited employment,[14] or a motion presented for harassment or other improper purpose.[15] Most trial judges are reluctant to entertain disqualification motions premised solely on suspected improper solicitation, but when clear evidence of such improper conduct exists, the judge may have no alternative but to take appropriate action. Indeed, a judge could be subject to judicial discipline if the judge fails to report the matter to disciplinary authorities "or take other appropriate action."[16]

---

[14] *Cf.* Tex. R. Civ. P. 192 cmt. 1 ("While the scope of discovery is quite broad, it is nevertheless confined by the subject matter of the case and *reasonable expectations* of obtaining information that will *aid resolution* of the dispute.") (emphasis added).

[15] *See generally* Tex. Civ. Prac. & Rem. Code § 10.001(1), (3) ("The signing of a pleading or motion . . . constitutes a certificate . . . that to the signatory's best knowledge, information, and belief, *formed after reasonable inquiry* . . . (1) the pleading or motion is *not being presented for any improper purpose, including to harass* or to cause unnecessary delay or needless increase in the cost of litigation . . . [and] (3) each allegation or other factual contention in the pleading or motion has evidentiary support or, for a specifically identified allegation or factual contention, is likely to have evidentiary support after a reasonable opportunity for further investigation or discovery . . . .") (emphasis added); *cf.* Texas Lawyer's Creed art. III.19 (stating that a lawyer is not to seek disqualification "unless it is necessary for the protection of my client's lawful objectives or is fully justified by the circumstances.").

[16] *See* Texas Code of Judicial Conduct, Canon IIID(2) ("A judge who receives information clearly establishing that a lawyer has committed a violation of the Texas Disciplinary Rules of Professional Conduct *should take appropriate action.* A judge having knowledge that a lawyer has committed a violation of the Texas Disciplinary rules of Professional Conduct that raises a substantial question as to the lawyer's honesty, trustworthiness or fitness as a lawyer in other respects *shall inform* the Office of the General Counsel of the State Bar of Texas [now, the Office of Chief Disciplinary Counsel] or *take other appropriate action.*") (emphasis added). Note that under the Code's definitions, the directive in the first sentence of Canon IIID(2) is merely aspirational, but violation of the obligation in the second sentence could result in "disciplinary action" against the judge. *See id.* Canon 8B(1), (2).

§ 15.5 Other rules.

Apart from the Disciplinary Rules, other rules sometimes provide a basis for disqualifying counsel. Lawyers who are licensed in other states and reside outside of Texas and who want to appear pro hac vice in a particular case in Texas must comply with Rule XIX of the Rules Governing Admission to the Bar of Texas, including paying the non-resident fee required by § 82.0361 of the Texas Government Code. On occasion disqualification motions have targeted non-resident lawyers who have violated those requirements. Rule XIX(e) also allows a court to revoke the permission to appear for a non-resident lawyer who engages in professional misconduct.

Additionally, Texas lawyers are subject to administrative suspension for failure to comply with other State Bar Rules, such as concerning payment of membership dues and occupation tax,[17] or mandatory continuing legal education,[18] or failure to comply with IOLTA rules.[19] These types of administrative suspensions have given rise to disqualification motions and sua sponte trial court disqualifications.

§ 15.6 Statutes and regulations.

Occasionally a specific statute or regulation may serve as a basis for disqualification. For example, in *In re Texas Windstorm Insurance Association*,[20] the trial judge disqualified lawyers representing TWIA, based in part upon a specific regulation

---

[17] *See* State Bar Rules, art. 3, § 5 (automatic suspension for failure to pay membership dues and other assessments).

[18] State Bar Rules, art. 12, § 8(E) (automatic suspension for failure to comply with MCLE requirements).

[19] *See* Rules Governing the Operation of the Texas Access to Justice Foundation, Rule 23(d) (immediate suspension for failure to fulfill IOLTA compliance requirements).

[20] 417 S.W.3d 119 (Tex. App.—Houston [1st Dist.] 2013, orig. proceeding).

concerning conflicts of interest for TWIA's counsel.[21] The regulation provided:

> If legal counsel accepts an engagement from the association to represent it in a dispute involving a policyholder claim against the association and fails to disclose a conflict of interest, as required in this clause, such legal counsel shall be barred for a period of five years, from the date on which the conflict of interest is disclosed to the association, from representing the association as legal counsel in any dispute involving a policyholder claim against the association.[22]

The trial judge concluded that the regulation was an "absolute bar" to the lawyer representing TWIA.[23] In a 2-1 decision, the court of appeals granted mandamus relief overturning the disqualification, but the majority opinion did not dispute the propriety of the trial court's interpretation of the regulatory conflict-of-interest provision. The majority opinion also did not dispute that the regulatory violation, if it occurred, would allow disqualification under Rule 1.15(a)(1), which requires a lawyer to withdraw from representation that would result in a violation of any "law."[24]

§ 15.7 Disqualification as an inherent-power sanction.

The Texas Supreme Court has recognized that "[c]ourts possess inherent power to discipline an attorney's behavior."[25]

---

[21] *Id.* at 126-27.

[22] 28 Tex. Admin. Code § 5.4001(b)(4)(C)(iii)(V) (2012) (Tex. Dep't of Ins., Texas Windstorm Insurance Ass'n Plan of Operation).

[23] *In re Texas Windstorm Insurance Association*, 417 S.W.3d. at 127.

[24] *Id.* at 140.

[25] *In re Bennett*, 960 S.W.2d 35, 40 (Tex. 1998). Note that the Joint Order

Courts imposing inherent-power sanctions have assessed a wide variety of sanctions, including not only compensatory attorney's fees and financial penalties, but also requirements of ethics training and CLE.[26] Nationally, many courts have recognized that disqualification is a permissible inherent-power sanction, when appropriate.[27] Undoubtedly Texas courts have

---

of the Texas Supreme Court and the Texas Court of Criminal Appeals adopting the Texas Lawyer's Creed expressly authorizes provides that "[c]ompliance with the[se] rules depends . . . when necessary [on] enforcement by the courts through their inherent powers . . . ."

[26] *See, e.g., Kugle v. DaimlerChrysler Corp.*, 88 S.W.3d 355, 364-65 (Tex. App.—San Antonio 2002, pet. denied) (affirming an award of more than $865,000 in monetary sanctions); *Davis v. Rupe*, 307 S.W.3d 528, 531 (Tex. App.—Dallas 2010, no pet.) (affirming inherent-power sanctions against a lawyer, including a payment of $15,000 to opposing counsel and participation in 10 hours of ethics training; and stating that the "[inherent] power may be exercised to the extent necessary to deter, alleviate, and counteract bad faith abuse of the judicial process, such as any significant interference with the traditional core functions of the court. The core functions of a trial court include hearing evidence, deciding issues of fact raised by the pleadings, rendering final judgments, and enforcing judgments. Making misleading statements and misrepresentations to the court interferes with these core functions.") (citations omitted); *Kings Park Apts., Ltd. v. National Union Fire Ins. Co. of Pittsburgh, Pennsylvania*, 101 S.W.3d 525, 539-542 (Tex. App.—Houston [1st Dist.] 2003, pet. denied) (affirming inherent-power sanctions, including a requirement that the defendant place a copy of the Texas Lawyer's Creed in every litigation file and educate every litigation supervisor concerning the Creed).

[27] *See generally* Gregory P. Joseph, *Sanctions: The Federal Law of Litigation Abuse* § 28(B)(4), 541 (LexisNexis 5th ed. 2013) ("The courts have broad authority to discipline counsel for misconduct. That authority extends as far as suspension or disbarment from practice and includes the power to disqualify counsel from appearing in a litigation which he or she had conducted abusively."); *Lelsz v. Kavanagh*, 137 F.R.D. 646, 654-57 (N.D. Tex. 1991) (removing an Assistant Texas Attorney General from a case as a sanction for violations of a set of federal court standards similar to the Texas Lawyer's Creed).

the power to disqualify counsel for litigation misconduct and other misconduct, but thus far no reported decision upholding disqualification has relied solely on inherent-power sanctions.[28]

---

[28] *See generally In re Vossdale Townhouse Ass'n, Inc.*, 302 S.W.3d 890, 895-96 (Tex. App.—Houston [14th Dist.] 2009, orig. proceeding) (overturning a disqualification order issued against a lawyer who had engaged in discovery abuse by submitting 31,448 requests for admission and 1,136 requests for production; expressing "great empathy for the trial court's consternation and frustration with counsel's misguided strategy and tactics," but concluding that the circumstances did not overcome counsel's clients' right to choose counsel of their choice); *In re A.M.*, 974 S.W.2d 857, 863-64 (Tex. App.—San Antonio 1998, no pet.) (overturning the trial judge's disqualification order that prohibited a lawyer from representing a client in future proceedings relating to case, but stating that "[t]o the extent that the trial court's decision was based on [the lawyer's] improper tactics and involvement in the case, the call is closer. . . . There were accusations that [the lawyer], not [the client], was the impediment in normalizing family relationships. However, we cannot say that the record supports disqualification. The trial court's order was more a sanction for past behavior than it was a disqualification from present and future litigation."); *cf.* Tex. Gov't Code § 82.062 ("Any attorney who is guilty of . . . any fraudulent or dishonorable conduct, or malpractice may be suspended from practice, or the attorney's license may be revoked, by a district court of the county in which the attorney resides or in which the act complained of occurred.").

Chapter 16

Imputation and Screening

§ 16.1 Imputation and screening: in general.

As discussed above, Rules 1.06, 1.07, 1.08, and 1.09 generally impute disqualifying conflicts of interest to all lawyers[1] who are members of or associated with the law firm with a personally disqualified lawyer.[2] Texas generally does not allow law firms to screen the personally disqualified lawyer

---

[1] *See also* Tex. Comm. on Prof'l Ethics, Op. 598 (2010) (addressing imputed disqualification when an associate wanted to change firms but had represented a client on several breach-of-contract lawsuits in the first firm and the new firm was adverse to the client in another breach-of-contract case; and stating that "[i]f the new associate could not represent the law firm's client in the current litigation because of the associate's prior representation of the adverse party, the entire law firm would be prohibited from continuing the current representation. If the representation is prohibited, this prohibition would not be affected by the law firm's screening the newly hired associate from the current representation against the associate's former client.").

[2] *See* Rules 1.06(f), 1.07(e), 1.08(i) and 1.09(b), and §§ 4.6 and 5.7, above. *See also* Tex. Comm. on Prof'l Ethics, Op. 644 (2014) (addressing a conflict of interest that arose when a law clerk (X) worked on a case at one law firm (Firm A), and later when the law clerk became licensed to practice law, went to work for the law firm (Firm B) that was on the other side of the case; and concluding that Rule 1.09 would not require disqualification because X "was not a lawyer at Firm A and therefore did not personally represent" the party even though he had worked on the matter; but concluding that representation by Firm B "would violate Rule 1.06(b)(2) because the representation . . . would reasonably appear to be adversely limited by . . . X's responsibilities to his former employer Firm A and to [the now opposing party] and by . . . X's own interests in avoiding claims for misuse of confidential information previously entrusted to him"; that the conflict was nonconsentable under Rule 1.06(c)(1) because X could not "reasonably believe" that his representation of Firm B's client "would not be materially affected by" his obligations to Firm A and its client; and that under Rule 1.06(f), no other lawyer at Firm B could represent the client; and that screening would not avoid the imputed conflict).

in order to avoid imputed disqualification of the entire firm.[3] The exceptions are in Rules 1.10 and 1.11, concerning lawyers who formerly held governmental or adjudicatory positions. Those rules allow limited screening. The other principal exception is for nonlawyer employees of law firms; screening is permissible for nonlawyers.[4] Additionally, law firms and their clients sometimes enter voluntary screening agreements when lawyers (or law clerks) move from one firm to another.[5] Motions to disqualify commonly arise in the "migratory foul" setting—when a lawyer or nonlawyer moves from one firm to another.

§ 16.2 Imputation under Rules 1.06, 1.07, and 1.08.

Rules 1.06(f), 1.07(e), and 1.08(i) contain identical imputation language: "If a lawyer would be prohibited by this Rule from engaging in particular conduct, no other lawyer while a member of or associated with that lawyer's firm may engage in that conduct."[6] Under the "associated with" standard, disqual-

---

[3] By contrast, Model Rule 1.10(a) permits limited screening for former-client conflicts that arise from a lawyer's association with a prior firm. The lawyer must be "timely screened" from the matter and not receive any of the fee. Additionally, the former client must promptly receive written notice, including a description of the screening procedures, a statement that the firm is complying with the Rule, and notice that review "may be available before a tribunal." The screened lawyer and a law firm partner also must provide certification of compliance with the screening at "reasonable intervals," if the former client so requests, and on termination of the screening procedures. Under Model Rule 1.10(a)(1) imputation does not apply if the conflict results from a "personal interest" of the disqualified lawyer and does not pose a "significant risk of materially limiting" the representation of the client by other lawyers in the firm. *See also* Chapter 18, concerning the different approach followed in certain federal courts in Texas.

[4] *See* Chapter 13.

[5] *See also* Chapter 18, concerning the different imputation rules followed in federal court.

[6] By comparison, Model Rule 1.10 refers to lawyers "associated in a firm."

ification issues could apply to lawyers who are "of counsel," cocounsel, contract lawyers, or who share office space.[7]

§ 16.3 Imputation under Rule 1.09.

Rule 1.09 has two imputation provisions. Rule 1.09(b) generally provides that when Rule 1.09(a) bars any individual lawyer from representing a client against a former client, no other lawyer in the firm or associated with the firm may undertake the representation. The express exception is if Rule 1.10 (concerning successive government and private employment) allows the representation.[8]

On the other hand, Rule 1.09(c) addresses what happens when a personally-prohibited lawyer leaves a law firm. In that event the firm is generally free to undertake representation adverse to the former client except in two situations.[9] The rationale for allowing the representation adverse to the former client in that situation is that the threat of disclosure or adverse use of the former client's confidential information ends when the lawyer who has the information leaves the firm. But the first excep-

---

[7] See In re CMH Homes, Inc., 2013 WL 2446724, at *5 (Tex. App.—San Antonio 2013, orig. proceeding) (construing the phrase "associated with" under Rule 1.09(b), stating that the common meaning of the term "associated" is "closely connected (as in function or office) with another," and concluding that "[w]ith this definition in mind, we construe Rule 1.09(b) to include not only partners, employees, and associates within the same firm, but individuals working together on a case or issue regardless of their actual status as a member of the firm, of-counsel, or cocounsel. To hold to the contrary, that Rule 1.09(b) only applies to actual employees of the same law firm, would amount to disregarding the plain and common meaning of 'associate with.'"). See also § 10.2, above, concerning cocounsel disqualification.

[8] See § 16.7 below.

[9] See Rule 1.09 cmt. 7 ("If . . . a lawyer disqualified by paragraph (a) should leave a firm, paragraph (c) prohibits lawyers remaining in that firm from undertaking representation that would be forbidden to the departed lawyer *only if* that representation would violate subparagraphs (a)(1) or (a)(2)." (emphasis added)).

tion to that principle is that the firm and its lawyers may not undertake new representation that would violate Rule 1.09(a)(1)—that is, if the new client or matter would "question[] the validity of the lawyer's services or work product for the former client." The second exception is that representation also is impermissible if it would violate Rule 1.09(a)(2)—that is, if the representation "in reasonable probability" would result in a violation of the confidentiality rule, Rule 1.05.

Evidence in disqualification hearings sometimes focuses on a threat to former-client confidentiality even after the personally-prohibited lawyer has left the firm. While the departing lawyer may have had the most knowledge of the client's confidential information, other lawyers may have had significant or even incidental exposure to the former client's confidential information. For example, a billing partner may have reviewed the bills sent to the client. Or the departing lawyer may have discussed the client's case at firm litigation-section or marketing-committee meetings. And often the departing lawyer may leave substantial confidential information on the firm's computer system or other firm databases. Again, these inquiries can be fact-intensive.

A lawyer who leaves the firm and did not personally represent the former client or obtain that client's confidential information is in a different position. Comment 7 to the Rule provides that that lawyer generally may "undertake representation against the lawyer's former client unless prevented from doing so by" another rule.[10]

---

[10] *See also* Tex. Comm. on Prof'l Ethics, Op. 527 (1999) (discussing and summarizing when representation may be proper or improper in the departing-lawyer context); Tex. Comm. on Prof'l Ethics, Op. 501 (1995); *In re Proeducation Int'l, Inc.*, 587 F.3d 296, 301-03 (5th Cir. 2009) (holding that the trial court erred in disqualifying the challenged lawyer who left the firm without having represented the client or obtained confidential client information; stating that "[u]nder Texas Rule 1.09(b), Kennedy was conclusively disqualified by imputation from representing D'Andrea

§ 16.4 Screening: in general.

Texas decisions allow screening to avoid imputation of conflicts of interest (and therefore disqualification) in only limited situations, principally involving (1) nonlawyer employees,[11] (2) lawyers who have successive government and private employment (Rule 1.10), and (3) lawyers who have served as adjudicatory officials or law clerks (Rule 1.11). Otherwise, screening a conflicted lawyer generally will not avoid imputation of the conflict to the entire firm.[12]

Screening usually refers to concurrent conflicts and former-client conflicts. But related doctrines apply to other rules that provide grounds for disqualification.[13] For example, Rule 3.08, the lawyer-as-witness rule, has a quasi-screening exception to the general prohibition against a lawyer acting as both advocate and witness before the tribunal. If the Rule's prohibition reaches one lawyer in a firm, then with the client's consent another lawyer in the firm may act as an advocate if the prohibited lawyer does not take an "active role before the tribunal in the presentation of the matter." The Rule does not require complete screening of the prohibited lawyer. As Comment 7 states, the prohibited lawyer may continue to participate in the

---

only while he remained at Jackson Walker. When Kennedy ended his affiliation with Jackson Walker without personally acquiring confidential information about MindPrint, his imputed disqualification also ended"; and concluding that the same result would apply under both the Texas Rules and the Model Rules because "both require that a departing lawyer must have actually acquired confidential information about the former firm's client or personally represented the former client to remain under imputed disqualification" (citing Op. 501 and Comment 7 to Rule 1.09)).

[11] See Chapter 13.

[12] Note that some federal decisions have followed a different approach, allowing screening of lawyers. See Chapter 18.

[13] See Chapters 10 and 11, concerning disqualification of cocounsel and successor counsel.

preparation of the case.[14]

§ 16.5 Screening of nonlawyers.

In part because of concern that disqualification could "unduly restrict" the mobility of nonlawyers,[15] the Texas Supreme Court has applied different standards to nonlawyers and has allowed screening. Nonetheless, if "a serious conflict of interest is present because of a nonlawyer's work on a matter that the nonlawyer previously worked on for opposing counsel, important public policies may balance in favor of disqualification."[16]

---

[14] *See* Chapter 8.

[15] *See In re Columbia Valley Healthcare Syst., L.P.*, 320 S.W.3d 819, 825-26 (Tex. 2010) ("We have stated that, as compared to lawyers, there is greater concern that the mobility of nonlawyers could be 'unduly restricted.' . . . Further, a nonlawyer employee may not have the same financial interest in the results of a case, nor the same understanding of confidential information as a lawyer." (citations omitted)).

[16] *Id. See In re American Home Prods. Corp.*, 985 SW.2d 68, 76 (Tex. 1998) (disqualifying law firm because it failed to rebut presumption that a nonlawyer shared confidential information with the new firm); *Phoenix Founders, Inc. v. Marshall*, 887 S.W.2d 831, 836 (Tex. 1994) (remanding for the trial court to determine whether the law firm had effectively screened the nonlawyer); *Grant v. Thirteenth Court of Appeals*, 888 S.W.2d 466, 468 (Tex. 1994) (requiring disqualification because of ineffective screening); *In re SAExploration, Inc.*, 2012 WL 6017717 (Tex. App.—Houston [14th Dist.] 2012, orig. proceeding) (upholding disqualification of an in-house counsel because of lack of effective screening; applying the nonlawyer-disqualification standards because the in-house counsel was not acting as a lawyer on the matter, but rather as a corporate officer); *In re Barnes*, 2003 WL 1848763, at *1 (Tex. App.—Beaumont 2003, orig. proceeding) (concluding that the screening was effective); *In re Bell Helicopter Textron, Inc.*, 87 S.W.3d 139, 145-48 (Tex. App.—Fort Worth 2002, orig. proceeding [mand. denied]) disapproved of by *In re RSR Corp.*, 2015 WL 7792871 (Tex. 2015) (applying the nonlawyer-disqualification standards to disqualify a consulting expert who was a former Bell employee, and had not worked on the present case, but had worked on cases involving the same model helicopter, and who had not been effectively screened); *but cf. In re Guaranty Ins. Servs., Inc.*, 343 S.W.3d 130, 136-37 (Tex. 2011)

The disqualifying presumptions work differently for nonlaw-yers. Two "conclusive," irrebuttable presumptions normally apply to lawyers who have worked on a matter and then switch to another firm that is on opposite side of the matter: (1) at the first firm, the lawyer *received* confidential information; (2) at the second firm, the lawyer *shared* the confidential infor-mation.[17] But for nonlawyers, only the first conclusive pre-sumption applies—that the nonlawyer who worked on a mat-ter *received* the confidential information at the first firm. The second presumption, concerning sharing, is rebuttable through "effective screening."[18]

Note that the screening procedures for nonlawyer staff do not apply to fact witnesses who have information about their for-mer employer if the former employer had not hired the em-ployee for litigation purposes and the employee's function was not primarily to report to lawyers.[19]

(disqualification not required even though the screening failed, despite the second firm's "exemplary" efforts, because the nonlawyer did not disclose confidential information, the second firm had "taken measures to reduce the potential for misuse of confidences to an acceptable level," and no evidence showed that the supervising lawyer "reasonably should have known about the conflict"); *Rubin v. Enns*, 23 S.W.3d 382, 388-89 (Tex. App.—Amarillo 2000, orig. proceeding [mand. denied]) (concluding that screening was effective); *Arzate v. Hayes*, 915 S.W.2d 616, 620 (Tex. App.—El Paso 1996, writ dism'd) (holding that the screening was effective).

[17] See Chapter 4, above. *See also Phoenix Founders, Inc. v. Marshall*, 887 S.W.2d 831, 833-34 (Tex. 1994).

[18] *See Columbia Valley Healthcare Syst., L.P.*, 320 S.W.3d 819, 828-29 (Tex. 2010) (disqualifying attorney because of inadequate screening of legal assistant); *see also* Restatement §123 cmt. f. (generally treating law students the same as other nonlawyer employees, unless special circumstances apply; but, for imputation purposes, treating former students who have finished law school but are awaiting admission to practice as lawyers).

[19] *See In re RSR Corp.*, 2015 WL 7792871 (Tex. 2015); *see also* Chapter 12, above.

§ 16.6 Screening: determining whether screening is effective.

Because Texas case law generally does not allow screening of lawyers, most reported court decisions that have analyzed the effectiveness of screening have focused on nonlawyer screens. The analysis is fact-specific. Factors that courts have analyzed include:

- whether the new firm instructed the nonlawyer "not to perform work on any matter on which she worked during her prior employment, or regarding which [she] has information related to her former employer's representation";[20]

- whether the new firm took "other reasonable steps to ensure that the [nonlawyer] does not work in connection with matters on which the [nonlawyer] during the prior employment";[21]

- the "substantiality of the relationship between the former and current matters";[22]

- the "time elapsing between the matters";[23]

- the "size of the firm";[24]

---

[20] *In re Columbia Valley Healthcare Syst., L.P.*, 320 S.W.3d 819, 824 (Tex. 2010).

[21] *Id.*; *Phoenix Founders, Inc. v. Marshall*, 887 S.W.2d 831, 835 (Tex. 1994); *Grant v. Thirteenth Court of Appeals*, 888 S.W.2d 466, 467-68 (Tex. 1994).

[22] *In re Columbia Valley Healthcare Syst., L.P.*, 320 S.W.3d 819, 824-25 (Tex. 2010).

[23] *Id.*

[24] *Id.* As a practical matter, screening may be more much difficult to achieve in a small firm than in a multinational firm in which staff in one office may have very little contact with staff in other offices.

- the "number of individuals presumed to have confidential information";[25]

- the nature of the nonlawyer's involvement in the former matter;[26]

- the timing of steps taken to reduce the risk of disclosure.[27]

For example, in *Rubin v. Enns*,[28] the court of appeals approved the law firm's screening procedures. Those procedures included the following steps:

- the managing partner of the firm sent a memo to all lawyers and staff (1) identifying the two cases on which the legal assistant might have confidential information, (2) instructing recipients that the disciplinary rules prohibited the legal assistant from disclosing any information concerning the cases, and (3) stating that any violation of the screening procedures would be grounds for termination;

- the firm prohibited the legal assistant from working on or discussing the two cases, or disclosing any information concerning the cases;

- the firm removed all computer information concerning the cases from the firm computer systems;

- the case files were stored in a limited-access, locked file cabinet in the managing partner's office, and the

---

[25] *Id.* Because of shared servers and cloud computing, access to data throughout the law firm is common.

[26] *Id.*

[27] *Id.*

[28] 23 S.W.3d 382 (Tex. App.—Amarillo 2000, orig. proceeding [mand. denied]).

files had to be returned to that location at the end of each business day;

- the managing partner met with each employee and obtained written agreement from each to comply with the screening procedures.

Screening after the fact is generally inadequate. The presumption of shared confidences "becomes conclusive" if:

(1) information relating to the representation of an adverse client has in fact been disclosed;

(2) screening would be ineffective or the nonlawyer necessarily would be required to work on the other side of a matter that is the same or substantially related to a matter on which the nonlawyer has previously worked, or

(3) the nonlawyer has actually performed work, including clerical work, on the matter at the lawyer's directive if the lawyer reasonably should have known about the conflict of interest.[29]

Ordinarily, when a screen fails, disqualification results. However, in an unusual decision, the Texas Supreme Court in *In re Guaranty Ins. Servs., Inc.*,[30] held that disqualification was unnecessary even when the screening did not fully succeed. The court overturned the trial court's disqualification of a law firm, Strasburger & Price, that had hired a paralegal who previously had worked at a firm that had represented the opposing party in a current case. Strasburger had taken these steps:

---

[29] *In re Columbia Valley Healthcare Syst., L.P.*, 320 S.W.3d 819, 825-827 (Tex. 2010).

[30] 343 S.W.3d 130 (Tex. 2011).

- It ran what the court of appeals called an "exemplary" conflicts check. That check identified the paralegal's former law-firm employer. The former employer did not represent the opposing party at the time of the conflicts check.

- The firm interviewed the paralegal, but he was unaware of a conflict and did not recall having worked 6.8 hours on the underlying suit at the former firm.

- During the paralegal's orientation, the firm instructed him to notify the firm if he became aware of a matter on which he had worked during his previous employment. The same instruction appeared in the firm's employee handbook and in a confidentiality agreement he signed.[31]

Despite those precautions, the paralegal worked on the underlying suit at Strasburger, billing 27 hours. When opposing counsel recognized the paralegal's name on an email and notified Strasburger, the firm immediately instructed the paralegal to stop work on the matter, to not view or access any documents in the case, and to not disclose any information he had received during his prior employment.[32]

In overturning Strasburger's disqualification, the supreme court stated that "in most cases, disqualification is not required if 'the practical effect of formal screening has been achieved.'"[33] Strasburger had taken "measures sufficient to reduce the potential for misuse of confidences to an acceptable level"[34] and thereby avoided disqualification.

---

[31] *Id.* at 132-33.

[32] *Id.* at 133.

[33] *Id.* at 134 (citation omitted).

[34] *Id.* at 134-35.

§ 16.7 Screening under Rules 1.10 and 1.11.

Rule 1.10 and Rule 1.11 expressly allow limited screening.[35] Rule 1.10 generally prohibits a lawyer from representing a private client in a matter in which the lawyer "participated personally and substantially as a public officer or employee" unless the governmental agency consents.[36] Rule 1.10(b) imputes that disqualification to others in that lawyer's firm, but permits the firm to undertake or continue the representation if the disqualified lawyer is "screened from any participation in the matter and is apportioned no part of the fee therefrom."[37] Rule 1.11(b), concerning former adjudicatory officials and law clerks, uses nearly identical language on screening and nonapportionment of fee.[38]

Rule 1.10(d) allows similar screening in the situation addressed by Rule 1.10(c): the situation in which a government lawyer acquires confidential information about a person, and then later considers representing a private client with interests adverse to that person. The Rule bars such representation by the particular lawyer, unless a law expressly permits the representation. However, others in the firm may represent the private client if the disqualified lawyer is screened and is apportioned no part of the fee.

---

[35] *See* Chapters 6 and 7, above.

[36] Rule 1.10(a).

[37] Rule 1.10(b)(2) also requires reasonably prompt written notice to the government agency. However, the firm may delay giving the notice if premature disclosure would injure the client. Rule 1.10 cmt. 6. But notice must be "as soon as practicable," to give the agency a reasonable opportunity to take appropriate action. *Id.*

[38] *See* Rule 1.11(b). In addition to the requirements for screening and non-apportionment of fee, Rule 1.11(c)(2) requires prompt written notice to the other parties in the proceeding. *See also In re de Brittingham*, 319 S.W.3d 95, 101 (Tex. App.—San Antonio 2010, orig. proceeding) (disqualifying a former appellate judge and her law firm under Rule 1.11 because she had participated in a related case when she was on the court; also concluding that disqualification did not require a showing of prejudice).

Chapter 17

Waiver of Disqualification

§ 17.1 Waiver by Delay.

A party may waive a motion to disqualify by delay.[1] For example, in *Vaughan v. Walther*[2] the Texas Supreme Court granted mandamus relief to overturn disqualification when the movant delayed six and one-half months before seeking disqualification.

While Texas courts have not set a specific deadline for filing a motion to disqualify, a six-month delay—or even less—can prove fatal.[3] On the other hand, a delay of one or two months is usually insufficient to establish waiver.[4]

---

[1] *Grant v. Thirteenth Court of Appeals*, 888 S.W.2d 466, 468 (Tex. 1994) ("A party that fails to seek disqualification timely waives the complaint.") (citing *HECI Exploration Co. v. Clajon Gas Co.*, 843 S.W.2d 622, 628-29 (Tex. App.—Austin 1992, writ denied)).

[2] 875 S.W.2d 690, 691 (Tex. 1994).

[3] *See Buck v. Palmer*, 381 S.W.3d 525, 528 (Tex. 2012) (waiver by seven-month delay); *In re La. Tex. Healthcare Mgmt., LLC,* 349 S.W.3d 688, 690-91 (Tex. App.—Houston [14th Dist.] 2011, orig. proceeding) (waiver by 13-month delay); *HECI Exploration Co. v. Clajon Gas Co.*, 843 S.W.2d 622, 628-29 (Tex. App.—Austin 1992, writ denied) (waiver by 11-month delay); *Conoco, Inc. v. Baskin,* 803 S.W.2d 416, 420 (Tex. App.—El Paso 1991, orig. proceeding) (holding that trial judge could have reasonably found waiver when motion to disqualify was filed 11-months after conflict discovered, and one and one-half months before trial); *Enstar Petroleum Co. v. Mancias*, 773 S.W.2d 662, 664 (Tex. App.—San Antonio 1989, orig. proceeding) (waiver by three-month delay).

[4] *Wasserman v. Black,* 910 S.W.2d 564, 568-69 (Tex. App.—Waco 1995, orig. proceeding); *see also In re American Home Prods. Corp.*, 985 S.W.2d 68, 73 (Tex. 1998) ("The record reflects that Wyeth made diligent efforts to depose all of plaintiffs' experts, including Dr. Gonzalez. Even if the date of his designation could be used as the benchmark for notice to Wyeth, which it cannot, the delay in filing the motion to disqualify, which was less than two months, as a matter of law did not constitute a waiver under the

Courts consider "the length of time between the moment the conflict became apparent to the aggrieved party to the time the motion for disqualification is filed."[1]

Because Texas courts discourage use of motions to disqualify as "tactical weapon[s],"[2] some courts have considered evidence showing that the motion is being used solely to delay litigation.[3]

§ 17.2 Other Waivers.

While delay is the most common basis for waiver, other types of waiver are possible. For example, the Texas Supreme Court has suggested that a movant might waive disqualification by failing to seek a stay of proceedings in the trial court while a motion for rehearing was pending in the Texas Supreme Court.[4] Parties opposing disqualification have argued various

---

facts of this case."); *In re Taylor,* 67 S.W.3d 530, 534 (Tex. App.—Waco 2002, orig. proceeding) (two-and-one-half-month delay was not waiver); *Syntek Finance Corp. v. Metropolitan Life Ins. Co.,* 880 S.W.2d 26, 34 (Tex. App.—Dallas 1994), *rev'd on other grounds,* 881 S.W.2d 319 (Tex. 1994) (six-week delay was not waiver);.

[1] *Wasserman v. Black,* 910 S.W.2d 564, 568 (Tex. App.—Waco 1995, orig. proceeding).

[2] *See, e.g., Spears v. Fourth Court of Appeals,* 797 S.W.2d 654, 658 (Tex. 1990) (stating that a party's motion to disqualify counsel had "all the appearances of a tactical weapon").

[3] *See, e.g., In re La. Tex. Healthcare Mgmt., LLC,* 349 S.W.3d 688, 690 (Tex. App.—Houston [14th Dist.] 2011, orig. proceeding) (citing *Spears v. Fourth Court of Appeals,* 797 S.W.2d 654, 656 (Tex. 1990)).

[4] *See Henderson v. Floyd,* 891 S.W.2d 252, 254-55 (Tex. 1995) (stating that the trial court should address that argument as a factual issue); *cf. In re Yarn Processing Patent Validity Litig.,* 530 F.2d 83, 90 (5th Cir. 1976) ("The underlying rules relating to attorney conflicts of interest are designed to allay any apprehension a client may have in frank discussion of confidential information with his attorney. Public confidence in the privacy of this discussion should not be impaired where the former client, having every opportunity to do so, fails to object to a new relationship involving his former attorney, and where the unethical nature of the attorney's change

other forms of waiver, estoppel, and implied consent.[5]

§ 17.3 Explaining Delay.

In evaluating waiver-by-delay arguments, some decisions have excluded periods during which parties have attempted to learn the facts and resolve disqualification issues through negotiations.[6]

---

of sides is not manifest but would need to be shown.").

[5] *See, e.g., Consolidated Theatres, Inc. v. Warner Bros. Circuit Mgt. Corp.*, 216 F.2d 920, 926 (2d Cir. 1954) ("The appellant . . . refers to other instances in which lawyers without challenge have accepted retainers by exhibitors to sue distributors whom they theretofore had professionally represented. But for aught that we can tell the absence of challenge in those cases was attributable to an implied consent by the clients to the adverse representation . . . .") (cited in *In re Yarn Processing Patent Validity Litig.*, 530 F.2d 83, 89 (5th Cir. 1976)).

[6] *See, e.g., In re EPIC Holdings*, 985 S.W. 2d 41, 52-53 (Tex. 1998) (refusing to find waiver from a seven-month delay between when movants learned of allegedly disqualifying facts and when they filed the motion to disqualify, because for at least four months, the movants had worked with the other party to identify and try to resolve disqualification issues); *In re Hoar Constr., L.L.C.*, 256 S.W.3d 790, 796-98 (Tex. App.—Houston [14th Dist.] 2008, orig. proceeding) (a party attempted to resolve disqualification issues before filing the disqualification motion, and the court concluded that a two-month delay did not waive the motion); *Rio Hondo Implement Co. v. Euresti*, 903 S.W.2d 128, 131 (Tex. App.—Corpus Christi 1995, orig. proceeding) (a three-month delay between when a party learned about the conflict and the party filed the disqualification motion did not waive the disqualification, when the party spent two and one-half months attempting to resolve the issue).

Chapter 18

Disqualification In Federal Court

§ 18.1 Introduction.

Disqualification standards can vary between state and federal courts. For example, while the Texas courts look to the Texas Disciplinary Rules of Professional Conduct for "guidance" in ruling on motions to disqualify,[1] the Fifth Circuit Court of Appeals follows the ethical rules "announced by the national profession in light of the public interest and the litigants' rights."[2]

As a practical matter, in federal courts that difference generally requires analyzing disqualification issues under both the Texas Rules and the ABA Model Rules.[3] But in some federal cases, courts also have considered local court rules as well as the Restatement (Third) of the Law Governing Lawyers. The Fifth Circuit approach sometimes leads to a different result—or even an opposite result—from what would happen in state court.

As the Fifth Circuit stated in *Federal Deposit Ins. Corp. v. United States Fire Ins. Co.*[4]:

---

[1] *See* Chapter 3.

[2] *In re Dresser Indus. Inc.*, 972 F.2d 540, 543 (5th Cir. 1992).

[3] *See, e.g., In re ProEducation Int'l, Inc.*, 587 F.3d 296, 299 (5th Cir. 2009) ("[T]he Texas Rules 'are not the sole authority governing a motion to disqualify.' A reviewing court also 'consider[s] the motion governed by the ethical rules announced by the national profession in light of the public interest and the litigants' rights.' The Fifth Circuit has recognized the ABA Model Rules of Professional Conduct (Model Rules) as the national standards to consider in reviewing motions to disqualify. Therefore, we shall consider both the Texas Rules and the Model Rules.") (citations omitted).

[4] 50 F.3d 1304 (5th Cir. 1995).

'[D]isqualification cases are governed by state and national ethical standards adopted by the court.' At least four separate ethical canons [sic] are relevant to a review of the district court's order to disqualify counsel in the instant case . . . . As authorized by 28 U.S.C. §2071, district courts . . . may adopt rules for the conduct of attorneys. The local rules promulgated by the local court itself are the most immediate source of guidance for a district court . . . . Nonetheless, parties cannot be deprived of the right to counsel of their choice on the basis of local rules alone. Local rules are not the 'sole' authority governing motions to disqualify counsel. Motions to disqualify are substantive motions. Therefore, they are decided under federal law. When reviewing the disqualification of an attorney, we must 'consider the motion governed by the ethical rules announced by the national profession in the light of the public interest and the litigant's rights.' The norms embodied in the Model Rules and the Model Code are relevant to our inquiry, 'as the national standard utilized by this circuit in ruling on disqualification motions.' Additionally, consideration of the Texas Rules is also necessary, because they govern attorneys practicing in Texas generally . . . .[5]

---

[5] *Id.* at 1311-12 (citations omitted). *See also Hill v. Hunt*, 2008 WL 4108120, at *2 (N.D. Tex. 2008) ("Although federal courts may adopt state or ABA rules as their ethical standards, whether and how those rules should be applied remains a question of federal law. Thus, while Texas Disciplinary Rules of Professional Conduct may be relevant to the issue of disqualification, these rules are not dispositive. The court views ABA and state rules and standards in light of the litigant's rights and the public interest, considering whether a conflict has the appearance of impropriety in general, or a possibility that a specific impropriety will occur, and the likelihood of public suspicion from the impropriety outweighs any social interest which would be served by the lawyer's continued participation in the case.") (citations omitted).

Indeed, in that decision the Fifth Circuit examined the Texas Rules, the Model Rules, the Model Code,[6] the local rules of the Northern District of Texas, and the Restatement.

§ 18.2 Federal court decisions.

Because the Texas Rules and the Model Rules differ, federal courts sometimes decide disqualification decisions differently than Texas courts would.[7] Examples include:

*In *In re Dresser Indus. Inc.*,[8] the trial judge denied a motion to disqualify, concluding that no substantial relationship existed between the antitrust case in which the law firm was suing Dresser and the two other cases in which the law firm was representing Dresser. The trial judge had analyzed the conflict under Texas Rule 1.06, which generally prohibits such simultaneous representation only if the matters are "substantially related." The Fifth Circuit held that the trial judge erred in relying on only the Texas Rules. Instead, applying "the ethical rules announced by the national profession in

---

[6] *But see Cramer v. Sabine Transp. Co.*, 141 F. Supp.2d 727, 729-30 (S.D. Tex. 2001) (rejecting reliance on the Model Code; stating "as the ABA adopted the Model Rules in 1983 as a replacement for the Model Code, the Model Code arguably no longer represents the ethical rules of the national profession.... Accordingly, this Court will look principally to the Model Rules and the Texas rules in addressing the question of disqualification.") (citations omitted); *Marin v. Gilberg*, 2008 WL 2770382, at *2 (S.D. Tex. 2008) (same).

[7] *See also* Tex. Comm. on Prof'l Ethics, Op. 645 (2014) ("For courts in the Fifth Circuit, including bankruptcy and other federal courts in Texas, the standard used in the case of conflicts of interest concerning a lawyer's current clients differs from that set forth in Rule 1.06 of the Texas Disciplinary Rules. The rule in the Fifth Circuit is that, in the absence of exceptional circumstances (which are not present in the facts considered in this opinion), a lawyer may not be adverse to a current client, except with the consent of both clients, regardless of whether the matters are substantially related and regardless of whether the representation could be expected to be adversely limited in any way by the representation of the adverse party in other matters.").

[8] 972 F.2d 540 (5th Cir. 1992).

light of the public interest and the litigants' rights," the Fifth Circuit examined the Model Rules, the Model Code, and the Restatement. The Fifth Circuit generally concluded that those "national standards" prohibited a lawyer from "bringing a suit against a current client without the consent of both clients."[9]

*In *Federal Deposit Ins. Corp. v. United States Fire Ins. Co.*,[10] a lawyer-as-witness conflict case, the Fifth Circuit reviewed the Texas Rules, the Model Rules, the Model Code, and the local rules of the Northern District of Texas. Ultimately on one issue the court opted for a standard inconsistent with the Texas Rules. Specifically, the court held that one of the lawyers in question should be disqualified, even though Texas Rule 3.08 would have authorized the lawyer to continue the representation if the client consented. Rejecting that Texas standard, the court stated that the "lawyer-witness rule enunciated in three of the four relevant ethical canons requires . . . disqualification."[11]

*In *National Oil Well Varco, L.P. v. Omron Oilfield & Marine, Inc.*,[12] the court refused to disqualify a law firm, even though the court recognized that the result would be the opposite in Texas state court. The court denied Omron's motion to disqualify lawyers in the firm (RB) that represented the plaintiff. Omron filed the motion after it discovered that Wunder, a lawyer at RB, had previously worked for the law firm Osha Liang (OL), which had represented Omron in what Omron argued were matters substantially related to the underlying patent infringement lawsuit. The court concluded that the conflict met the substantial-relationship test and that the first irrebuttable presumption applied—that is, the court recognized that the current and former representations involved substantially related matters, and the court therefore "irrebuttably presume[d]

---

[9] *Id.* at 544-45.

[10] 50 F.3d 1304 (5th Cir. 1995).

[11] *Id* at 1317.

[12] 60 F. Supp.3d 751 (W.D. Tex. 2014).

that relevant confidential information was disclosed during the former period of representation." Nonetheless, based upon a review of Fifth Circuit precedent, the court concluded that the second irrebuttable presumption that exists under Texas law—that the conflicted, migrating lawyer shares the former client's confidential information at the new law firm—did not apply. The court stated:

> In sum, under Fifth Circuit precedent, there is no established irrebuttable presumption a lawyer shares client confidences he possesses with other lawyers at his law firm. On the other hand, the Fifth Circuit has indicated in recent precedent . . . that, to the extent there is still a presumption . . . the presumption is rebuttable.[13]

*In *Galderama Laboratories, L.P. v. Actavis Mid-Atlantic LLC*,[14] the court identified the key issue as "whether or not Galderama, a sophisticated client, represented by in-house counsel, gave informed consent when it agreed to a general, open-ended waiver of future conflicts of interest in V&E's 2003 engagement letter."[15] The court analyzed the issue under Model Rule 1.7. The court observed that "[t]he Texas rule on conflicts of interest is more lenient than the Model Rule. . . . The difference between the Model Rule and the Texas Rule goes to the central issue in this case, the need for informed consent. To give weight to the Texas Rule over the Model Rule in this case would vitiate the cornerstone of the national standard, the requirement of informed consent. Thus, while the Court has considered the applicable Texas Rules, the Model Rules and authority related to them must control in determining Galderama's motion to disqualify."[16]

---

[13] *Id.* at *9.

[14] 927 F. Supp.2d 390 (N.D. Tex. 2013).

[15] *Id.* at 394 (citing *In re Dresser Indus. Inc.*, 972 F.2d 540, 543-45 (5th Cir. 1992)).

[16] *Id.* at 396.

*In *JuxtaComm-Texas Software, LLC v. Axway, Inc.*,[17] in analyzing a possible current-client conflict, the court stated that the "ABA Model Rules and the Texas Rules of Professional Conduct propound different tests for conflicts of interest arising in concurrent and former representations." The court noted that the Texas rule "requires not only that the clients are directly adverse but also that the matters are substantially related." However, because the "Fifth Circuit has shown a preference for the more stringent ABA Model Rule," the court selected the Model Rule approach.[18]

*In *Crossroad Systs. (Texas), Inc. v. Dot Hill Systs. Corp.*,[19] a lawyer-as-witness conflict case, the court disqualified a law firm. The court noted that the Model Rules would "allow members of the lawyer's firm to serve as trial counsel unless the conflict of interest rules would prohibit their service," but that the Texas Rules "are less forgiving as they prohibit other members of the firm from serving as trial counsel unless their client gives informed consent."[20] Nonetheless, the court held that because the "credibility and legal acumen" of the firm's lawyers would be challenged at trial, "under the circumstances presented here, a strict prohibition on all members of the testifying lawyer's firm serving as trial counsel is appropriate."[21]

---

[17] 2010 WL 4920909 (E.D. Tex. 2010).

[18] *Id.* at *2.

[19] 2006 WL 1544621 (W.D. Tex. 2006).

[20] *Id.* at *10.

[21] *Id.* at *11.

Chapter 19

Practical Tips for Disqualification

§ 19.1 Introduction. Deciding what steps to take in pursuing a motion to disqualify often depends upon the specific facts of the case, including the relationships among the parties and counsel, the stage of the proceedings, the movant's goals, the grounds for the motion, and available resources. For the most part, the steps to take in opposing disqualification are mirror-image tactics. The steps discussed below primarily relate to the most common types of motions to disqualify: current-client and former-client conflicts. Additional considerations may apply for motions relying on other grounds of disqualification.[1]

§ 19.2 Steps to take in seeking disqualification.

1. Act promptly.

As discussed above, delay in presenting a motion to disqualify counsel can result in waiver of the right to disqualify.[2] Thus, a party who learns of facts potentially giving rise to a basis for disqualification should act promptly to complete any necessary pre-motion investigation, and then, if a motion is appropriate, should file the motion and pursue it diligently.

2. Investigate the facts; consider negotiating the issues.

Disqualification proceedings can have important and adverse consequences for all parties and counsel in a case. The proceedings can be expensive and time-consuming. They can delay the resolution of

---

[1] *See* Chapters 8, 14, and 15.

[2] *See* Chapter 17.

the case. They can complicate communications and relationships among the parties and counsel.

When a possible disqualification issue first arises, the important controlling facts may be unknown or uncertain. Unless the matter is urgent, the party contemplating disqualification of opposing counsel ordinarily should investigate the issue fully before deciding whether to file a motion.

Sometimes investigation can be as simple as calling or writing opposing counsel to raise the concern and asking for an oral or written explanation of the facts.[3] If the opposing counsel can clarify the facts and allay the concerns, that may end the matter quickly and inexpensively.

As noted previously, in some waiver-by-delay situations, courts exclude from the "delay" period the time during which the parties reasonably attempt to discuss the possible disqualification issue, learn the underlying facts, and negotiate a mutually agreeable resolution.[4] However, if the potential movant decides to undertake such preliminary steps, the efforts should be documented. Moreover, it may be possible and advisable to negotiate a non-waiver agreement or standstill agreement, under which the parties agree to address the issues preliminarily before the motion is filed without prejudice to the potential movant from any period spent in that informal discovery and negotiation.

Most trial judges prefer to avoid disqualification hearings

---

[3] For example, a letter might start: "Dear [Counsel]: My client has learned facts indicating that your law firm may have a disqualifying conflict of interest. Before we take any action, we want to try learn all of the controlling facts and to give you the opportunity to explain the situation from your perspective. At present, it appears that Lawyer X in your firm formerly represented my client in a matter substantially related to the current case. [Etc.]."

[4] See Chapter 17.

and the contentiousness and hard feelings that often develop during those proceedings. Thus, another benefit of attempting to negotiate an agreed resolution is that the trial court may at least credit the movant with making a good-faith effort to avoid the necessity of a hearing.

A former-client movant may also need to obtain the client file from the former counsel as part of an investigation. In Texas, the client generally owns the file and is entitled to the file on request.[5] However, sometimes even a request for the file generates disagreement and delay.

Some disqualification motions go to hearing without any pre-hearing discovery. In other cases the parties may need to obtain substantial discovery, including depositions.

3. File an appropriately detailed motion.

It is not uncommon for parties to argue about whether a motion to disqualify is sufficiently detailed. On the one hand, the Texas Supreme Court has repeatedly stated that courts "must adhere to an exacting standard when considering motions to disqualify so as to discourage their use as a dilatory trial tactic."[6] On the other hand, as discussed above, the same

---

[5] *See generally* Rule 1.15(d) ("Upon termination of representation, a lawyer shall take steps to the extent reasonably practicable to protect a client's interests, such as . . . surrendering papers and property to which the client is entitled . . . ."); *In re McCann*, 422 S.W.3d 701, 705 (Tex. Crim. App. 2013) ("To whom does a client's file belong? The client's file belongs to the client."); *In re George*, 28 S.W.3d 511, 516 (Tex. 2000) (holding that "work product generated by the attorney in representing the client belongs to the client"); *Resolution Trust Corp. v. H__, PC*, 128 F.R.D. 647, 650 (N.D. Tex. 1989) (holding that a client has the right to the return of his papers, including legal memoranda and attorney notes); Tex. Comm. on Prof'l Ethics, Op. 570 (2006) (addressing the client's right to receive a lawyer's notes).

[6] *Spears v. Fourth Court of Appeals*, 797 S.W.2d 654, 656 (Tex. 1990); *accord In re NITLA S.A. de C.V.*, 92 S.W.3d 419, 422 (Tex. 2002); *Phoenix*

court has emphasized that the substantial-relationship test and related doctrines exist in part to "prevent the moving party from being forced to reveal the very confidences sought to be protected."[7]

As a starting point, the movant should specifically cite the bases of the motion—such as a concurrent-representation conflict under Rule 1.06, a former-client conflict under Rule 1.09, an anti-contact violation under Rule 4.02, etc. How many facts the movant will need to disclose in the motion then often becomes a balancing process, taking into account the competing considerations of providing fair notice and protecting confidentiality.

If the movant has engaged in pre-motion or pre-hearing discussions with the target lawyer to attempt to clarify the facts and negotiate a resolution, both sides will likely be aware of the central facts in issue. Additionally, a target lawyer who personally handled a prior or conflicting representation, for example, will usually be knowledgeable about the nature and details of that prior representation—and perhaps have more knowledge and access to documents and other relevant information than the movant.

4. Prepare and present evidence at the hearing.

Because disqualification determinations often are fact-intensive, and because the burden generally is on the movant to establish the grounds for disqualification, the movant should prepare to present the necessary testimony and exhibits. Appellate review, by mandamus or appeal, is not unusual. Therefore, the movant should ensure that the record on appeal will support disqualification. Of course, the movant also should make sure that the hearing is on the record.

Founders, Inc. v. Marshall, 887 S.W.2d 831, 836 (Tex. 1994).

[7] *Phoenix Founders, Inc. v. Marshall*, 887 S.W.2d 831, 834 (Tex. 1994).

It is often useful to provide the trial judge a brief or memorandum summarizing the key facts, as well as setting out the applicable legal standards.

5. Expert testimony.

Parties in disqualification hearings often present expert witnesses. Most trial courts allow the evidence, but some exclude it. As a practical matter, in a simple hearing before a trial judge who is experienced in hearing disqualification motions, expert testimony may be unnecessary. On the other hand, experts may have substantial background in conflict-of-interest and disqualification issues, and usually will attempt to identify and distill the parties' respective versions of how the applicable law applies to the controlling facts. Consequently, trial judges often find such evidence to be potentially informative and useful.

An issue that sometimes arises with experts is what evidence they review to prepare for the hearing. As discussed below, protection of the confidential information of a client or former client is often a central purpose of a motion to disqualify. The substantial-relationship test exists, in part, to protect the client or former client from having to disclose in the disqualification hearing the very confidential information that the client is seeking to protect in attempting to disqualify former counsel. Thus, the movant should be careful about what information the expert receives and discloses in testimony.

6. Protection of confidential information.

Frequently the most important reason to seek disqualification is to protect the confidential information of a client or former client. The lawyer or law firm that is the target of the disqualification motion possesses such information and may use the information in a way that is adverse and harmful to the client or former client. The substantial-relationship test focuses on the similarities of the two matters in order to help protect that confidential information. If the client were required to offer into evidence in open court the same confidential information that the client is trying to protect, the hearing could be pointless because the confidentiality would be destroyed.

Thus, the Texas Supreme Court and other appellate courts have repeatedly emphasized that the substantial-relationship test operates to "prevent the moving party from being forced to reveal the very confidences sought to be protected."[8]

The movant should take care to not unnecessarily disclose the very information sought to be protected. In some instances, that act of disclosure may rise to the level of waiver.

In some cases, trial courts permit, or even require, the movant to present certain confidential information—for example, to clarify the substantial-relationship between two matters—by *in camera* submission.[9] In most cases, however, the substantial-relationship test should make that procedure unnecessary and inadvisable.

7. Order.

The movant should prepare a draft Order for the trial judge to have available if the judge grants the motion to disqualify. Drafting such an Order raises issues concerning how detailed to make the findings in the Order and whether to have separate

---

[8] *Id.; see* Chapter 4.

[9] *See National Oil Well Varco, L.P. v. Omron Oilfield & Marine, Inc.,* 60 F. Supp.2d 751 (W.D. Tex. 2014) ("Omron, pursuant to this Court's order, also provided to the Court ex parte, under seal privileged emails, which constituted 'all of the privileged communications—of which Omron is aware—between Brian Wunder and Omron containing confidential information related to Osha Liang's work on a potential lawsuit filed against Omron by [NOV].'").

findings of fact.[10] That may depend on the facts and the grounds for disqualification, and a review of applicable caselaw before the hearing. For example, some decisions quote the language from *Coker*, that in proving a substantial relationship between two matters the movant should produce "evidence of specific similarities capable of being recited in the disqualification order."[11]

8. Appellate remedies.

If the trial court denies disqualification, the movant will need to consider seeking emergency relief in the court of appeals and mandamus relief.

§ 19.3 Steps to take in opposing disqualification.

The considerations discussed in § 19.2 above generally also apply to the party opposing the motion to disqualify.

If the opposing party or counsel raises the disqualification issue before filing a motion, it may be necessary to attempt to clarify the alleged basis of the threatened disqualification. A simple conversation with opposing counsel may dispel a misunderstanding and avoid the filing of a motion. Internal investigation within the firm and review of client documents also may clarify the dispute.

---

[10] *See In re RSR Corp.*, 405 S.W.3d 265, 271 n.3 (Tex. App.—Dallas 2013, orig. proceeding) *overruled sub nom. In re RSR*, 2015 WL 7792871 (Tex. 2015) ("Although the trial court's order disqualifying Bickel & Brewer contains various statements that could be interpreted as "fact findings," these "findings" do not constitute true "findings of fact" because they were not separately filed as required by Texas Rule of Civil Procedure 299a. *See* TEX.R. CIV. P. 299a (requiring findings of fact to be separately filed and not simply recited in judgment) .... Accordingly, we employ the standard of review applicable to cases where no findings have been requested or filed. ... In the absence of findings, we imply all necessary fact findings in support of the trial court's order.") (citations omitted).

[11] *See NCNB Tex. Nat'l Bank v. Coker*, 765 S.W.2d 398, 400 (Tex. 1989).

If the basis asserted for disqualification is valid, the target counsel should consult with the current client and opposing counsel to determine appropriate steps to take. In some cases, it may be possible to negotiate a contractual screening arrangement to remove the personally tainted counsel from any involvement in the case. If that lawyer previously had minimal exposure to confidential information in the case, that may provide satisfactory reassurance for the former client. On the other hand, if disqualification is likely, or if the target lawyer and client do not want to fight the issue, it's usually in the interest of all parties to arrange a smooth, timely, cooperative withdrawal, with adequate time for new counsel to appear and get up to speed, including a postponement of litigation deadlines, etc. If a co-counsel-conflict or successor-counsel-conflict issue arises, withdrawing counsel may also need to address appropriate protections to ensure that the conflict is not transferred to new counsel.[12]

If the targeted counsel and party decide to contest the motion to disqualify, they will need to analyze the legal grounds and facts asserted. If relevant evidence or issues are unknown or unclear, they may need to seek clarification from the movant and document that request. If the movant does not cooperate, they may need to file special exceptions and seek appropriate discovery to develop the necessary facts before the hearing.

Like the movant, the party opposing the motion to disqualify should consider preparing appropriate opposition and briefing on the issues; preparing for the evidentiary presentation at the hearing (including how to address the confidentiality issues); preparing expert testimony; analyzing waiver and timing issues; developing evidence concerning the motion being used for tactical abuse; and considering the specificity of any order or findings that the trial judge might issue.

---

[12] *See* Chapter 11.

If the trial court disqualifies counsel, that party should analyze whether to request a stay, and if the trial judge denies that relief, whether to seek immediate, emergency relief from the appellate courts to stay trial court proceedings. Then that party will need to decide whether to seek mandamus review or to raise the issue on appeal.

Chapter 20

List of Principal
Texas Decisions Addressing
Lawyer Disqualification

Texas Supreme Court cases

In re RSR Corp., 2015 WL 7792871 (Tex. 2015)
- Issue: Disqualification for receipt of confidential communication
- No disqualification

Buck v. Palmer, 381 S.W.3d 525 (Tex. 2012)
- Issue: Rule 1.09 — *Former-client conflict of interest*
- No disqualification

In re Guaranty Insurance Services, Inc., 343 S.W.3d 130 (Tex. 2011)
- Issue*: Disqualification for non-lawyer conflict*
- No disqualification

In re Columbia Valley Healthcare Syst., L.P., 320 S.W.3d 819 (Tex. 2010)
- Issue: *Rule 1.09 — Former-client conflict of interest*
- Disqualified

In re Basco, 221 S.W.3d 637 (Tex. 2007)
- Issue: *Rule 1.09 — Former-client conflict of interest*
- Disqualified

In re Cerberus Capital Management, L.P., 164 S.W.3d 379 (Tex. 2005)
- Issues: *Rule 1.05 - Disclosure of confidential information; Rule 1.09 — Former-client conflict of*

interest
- No disqualification

In re Sanders, 153 S.W.3d 54 (Tex. 2004*)*
- Issue: *Rule 3.08 — Lawyer as witness*
- No disqualification

In re Mitcham, 133 S.W.3d 274 (Tex. 2004*)*
- Issue: *Rule 1.09 — Former-client conflict of interest; Agreement regarding conflicts of interest*
- Disqualified

In re B.L.D., 113 S.W.3d 340 (Tex. 2003), *cert. denied*, 124 S. Ct. 1674 (2004)
- Issue: *Rule 1.06 — Concurrent conflict of interest*
- No disqualification

In re Nitla S.A. de C.V., 92 S.W.3d 419 (Tex. 2002*)*
- Issue: *Disqualification for receipt of confidential information*
- No disqualification

In re George, 28 S.W.3d 511 (Tex. 2000)
- Issue: *Successor counsel access prior attorney's confidential information and work product*
- Disqualified

In re American Home Prods. Corp., 985 S.W.2d 68 (Tex. 1998*)*
- Issues: *Disqualification for non-lawyer conflict*
- Disqualified

In re EPIC Holdings, Inc., 985 S.W.2d 41 (Tex. 1998)
- Issue: *Rule 1.09 — Former-client conflict of interest*
- Disqualified

In re Meador, 968 S.W.2d 346 (Tex. 1998)

- Issue: *Disqualification for receipt of confidential information; Disqualification for non-lawyer conflict*
- No disqualification

Anderson Producing, Inc. v. Koch Oil Co., 929 S.W.2d 416 (Tex. 1996)

- Issue: *Rule 3.08 — Lawyer as witness*
- No disqualification

Nat'l Med. Enters. v. Godbey, 924 S.W.2d 123 (Tex. 1996)

- Issue: *Rule 1.09 — Former-client conflict of interest; Rule 1.06 — Comment 6, Meaning of Directly Adverse; Express duty to preserve confidences to non-client (joint defense privilege)*
- Disqualified

Henderson v. Floyd, 891 S.W.2d 252 (Tex. 1995)

- Issue: *Rule 1.09 — Former-client conflict of interest, disqualification of law firm*
- Disqualified

Texaco, Inc. v. Garcia, 891 S.W.2d 255 (Tex. 1995)

- Issue: *Rule 1.09 — Former-client conflict of interest*
- Disqualified

Grant v. Thirteenth Court of Appeals, 888 S.W.2d 466 (Tex. 1994)

- Issue: *Disqualification for non-lawyer conflict*
- Disqualified

Metropolitan Life Ins. Co. v. Syntek Fin. Corp., 881 S.W.2d 319 (Tex. 1994)

- Issue: *Rule 1.09 — Former-client conflict of interest*
- No disqualification

Phoenix Founders, Inc. v. Marshall, 887 S.W.2d 831 (Tex. 1994)

- Issue: Disqualification for non-lawyer conflict
- No disqualification, *remanded for further consideration*

Vaughan v. Walther, 875 S.W.2d 690 (Tex. 1994)

- Issue: *Rule 1.09 — Former-client conflict of interest; Waiver of disqualification*
- No disqualification

Mauze v. Curry, 861 S.W.2d 869 (Tex. 1993)

- Issue: *Rule 3.08 — Lawyer as witness*
- Disqualified

Ayres v. Canales, 790 S.W.2d 554 (Tex. 1990)

- Issue: *Rule 3.08 — Lawyer as witness*
- No disqualification

Spears v. Fourth Court of Appeals, 797 S.W.2d 654 (Tex. 1990)

- Issue: *Rule 3.08 — Lawyers as witness; Rule 1.10 - Successive government & private employment*
- No disqualification

NCNB Tex. Nat'l Bank v. Coker, 765 S.W.2d 398 (Tex. 1989)

- Issue: *Rule 1.09 — Former-client conflict of interest*
- No disqualification

Texas Court of Criminal Appeals cases

State ex. rel. Young v. Sixth Judicial Dist. Court of Appeals, 236 S.W.3d 207 (Tex. Crim. App. 2007)

- Issue: *6th Amendment Right to Conflict-Free Representation*
- No disqualification

Gonzalez v. State, 117 S.W.3d 831 (Tex. Crim. App. 2003)

- Issue: *3.08 — Lawyer as witness*
- Disqualified

State ex rel. Eidson v. Edwards, 793 S.W.2d 1 (Tex. Crim. App. 1990)

- Issue: *Removal of Officials and Due Process, counterpart Rule 1.09 — Former-client conflict of interest*
- No disqualification

Texas Courts of Appeals cases

In re Getz, 2012 WL 2729639 (Tex. App.—Amarillo 2012, orig. proceeding)

- Issue: *Rule 3.08 — Lawyer as witness*
- Disqualified

In re Jackson, 2012 WL 2727869 (Tex. App.—Amarillo 2012, orig. proceeding)

- Issue: *Rule 1.09 — Former-client conflict of interest, co-counsel disqualification*
- Disqualified

In re Leyendecker, 2012 WL 3224108 (Tex. App.—Houston. [1st Dist.] 2012, orig. proceeding [mand. denied]) (mem. op.)

- Issue: *3.08 — Lawyer as witness*
- No disqualification

In re Reynoso, 361 S.W.3d 719 (Tex. App.—Corpus Christi 2012, orig. proceeding)

- Issue: *Duty to preserve confidences of a non-client (joint defense privilege)*
- Disqualified

In re Ryan, 2012 WL 6755005 (Tex. App.—Houston [1st Dist.] 2012, orig. proceeding)

- Issue: *Code of Judicial Conduct, Canons 1-4 (Family law attorney was an associate family law judge and without notice or hearing the trial court found there was a conflict of interest between her role as an attorney and her role as a judge); Due Process*
- No disqualification

In re SAExploration, Inc., 2012 WL 6017717 (Tex. App.—Houston [14th Dist.] 2012, no pet.)

- Issue: *Disqualification for non-lawyer conflict (lawyer employed as non-lawyer)*
- Disqualified

In re Louisiana Texas Healthcare Mgt., L.L.C., 349 S.W.3d 688 (Tex. App.—Houston [14th Dist.] 2011, orig. proceeding)

- Issue: *Waiver of disqualification*
- No disqualification

In re Brittingham, 319 S.W.3d 95 (Tex. App.—San Antonio 2010, orig. proceeding)

- Issue: *Rule 1.11 — Adjudicatory official or law clerk*
- Disqualified

French v. Law Offices of Wendel Turley, P.C., 2010 WL 744794 (Tex. App.—Fort Worth 2010, no pet.)

- Issue: *Rule 3.08 — Lawyer as witness*
- No disqualification

In re Guidry, 316 S.W.3d 729 (Tex. App.—Houston [14th Dist] 2010, orig. proceeding)

- Issue: *Rule 3.08 — Lawyer as witness*
- Disqualified

In re Mabray, 355 S.W.3d 16 (Tex. App.—Houston [1st Dist.] 2010, orig. proceeding [mand. denied])

- Issue: *(couple signed and filed a cooperative law agreement) Wife claims disqualification necessary because husband's attorney tried to contract around Texas' collaborative law statute with a cooperative law agreement.*
- No disqualification

Smith v. Abbott, 311 S.W.3d 62 (Tex. App.—Austin 2010, pet. denied)

- Issue: *Rule 1.10(c) - Successive government & private employment; Rule 7.03 — Prohibited solicitations and payments; Violation of separation agreement*
- Disqualified

In re Sandoval, 2009 WL 4891949 (Tex. App.—San Antonio 2009, orig. proceeding)

- Issue: *Rule 3.08 — Lawyer as witness*
- No disqualification

In re B.L.H., 2008 WL 864072 (Tex. App.—Houston [1st Dist.] 2008, no pet.) (mem. op.)

- Issue: *Rule 3.08 — Lawyer as witness*
- No disqualification

Carson v. State, 2008 WL 1867148 (Tex. App.—Fort Worth 2008, no pet.) (mem. op.)

- Issue: *Due Process Violation, counterpart Rule 1.09 — Former-client conflict of interest*
- No disqualification

In re Eagan, 2008 WL 739864 (Tex. App.—Dallas, 2008, orig. proceeding) (mem. op.)

- Issue: *Rule 1.09 — Former-client conflict of interest; Rule 3.08 — Lawyer as witness*
- No disqualification

In re Frost, 2008 WL 2122597 (Tex. App.—Tyler 2008, orig. proceeding [mand. denied]) (mem. op.)

- Issues: *Rule 1.09 — Former-client conflict of interest; Rule 3.08 — Lawyer as witness*
- No disqualification

In re Fulp, 2008 WL 1822758 (Tex. App.—Corpus Christi 2008, orig. proceeding) (mem. op.)

- Issue: *Rule 3.08 — Lawyer as witness*
- No disqualification

In re Hoar Constr., L.L.C., 256 S.W.3d 790 (Tex. App.—Houston [14th Dist.] 2008, orig. proceeding)

- Issue: *Rule 1.09 — Former-client conflict of interest*
- Disqualified

Klapesky v. State, 256 S.W.3d 442 (Tex. App.—Austin 2008, pet. ref'd)

- Issue: *6th Amendment Right to Conflict-Free Representation*
- Disqualified

In re Liberty Ins. Corp., 2008 WL 3925942 (Tex. App.—San Antonio 2008 [mand. denied]) (mem. op.)

- Issue: *Rule 1.09 — Former-client conflict of interest*
- No disqualification

In re State, 249 S.W.3d 675 (Tex. App.—Tyler 2008, orig. proceeding)

- Issue: *Rule 1.06 — Concurrent conflict of interest*
- No disqualification

Capital City Church of Christ v. Novak, 2007 WL 1501095 (Tex. App.—Austin 2007, no pet.)
- Issue: *Rule 1.09 — Former-client conflict of interest*
- No disqualification

In re Martel, 2007 WL 43616 (Tex. App.—Tyler, 2007, orig. proceeding) (mem. op.)
- Issue: *Rule 1.06 — Concurrent Conflict of Interest; Rule 3.08 - Lawyer as witness*
- No disqualification

SouthTex 66 Pipeline Co., Ltd. v. Spoor, 2007 WL 3071416 (Tex. App.—Houston [14th Dist.] 2007, pet. denied)
- Issue: *Rule 3.08 — Lawyer as witness*
- No disqualification, *affidavit held inadmissible*

In re A.L.S., 2006 WL 75369 (Tex. App.—Beaumont 2006, orig. proceeding)
- Issue: Rule 3.08 — Lawyer as witness
- No disqualification

In re Bennett, 2006 WL 2403319 (Tex. App.—Houston [14th Dist.] 2006, orig. proceeding) (mem. op.)
- Issue: *Rule 3.08 — Lawyer as witness*
- No disqualification

Cimarron Agric., Ltd. v. Guitar Holding Co., L.P., 209 S.W.3d 197 (Tex. App.—El Paso 2006, no pet.)
- Issue: *Rule 1.09 — Former-client conflict of interest*
- Disqualified in this case, overturned trial court's disqualification for any future representation

In re Dalco, 186 S.W.3d 660 (Tex. App.—Beaumont 2006, orig. proceeding [mand. denied])
- Issue: *Rule 1.05 - Confidentiality of information*

- No disqualification

In re Drake, 195 S.W.3d 232 (Tex. App.—San Antonio 2006, orig. proceeding [mand. denied])
- Issue: *Rule 1.05 - Confidentiality of information; Rule 1.09 — Former-client conflict of interest*
- No disqualification

In re Englehardt, 2006 WL 2640415 (Tex. App.—Houston [1st Dist.] 2006, orig. proceeding) (mem. op.)
- Issue: *Rule 1.09 — Former-client conflict of interest*
- Disqualified

Lopez v. Sandoval, 2006 WL 417326 (Tex. App.—Corpus Christi 2006, no pet.) (mem. op.)
- Issue: *Rule 1.09 — Former-client conflict of interest*
- No disqualification

In re McDaniel, 2006 WL 408397 (Tex. App.—Waco 2006, orig. proceeding) (mem. op.)
- Issue: *Rule 1.09 — Former-client conflict of interest; Rule 3.08 — Lawyer as witness*
- No disqualification

In re Parnham, 2006 WL 2690306 (Tex. App.—Houston [1st Dist.] 2006, orig. proceeding)
- Issue: *Texas Rule of Civil Procedure 193.3, counterpart Receipt of confidential information*
- No disqualification

In re Bivins, 162 S.W.3d 415 (Tex. App.—Waco 2005, orig. proceeding)
- Issues: *Rule 1.05 — Confidentiality of information; Rule 1.09 — Former-client conflict of interest; 3.08 — Lawyer as witness*
- No disqualification

Dean Park & Constr. & Real Estate Inv. Corp. v. Meredeith, Donnell & Abernethy, 2005 WL 1832046 (Tex. App.—Corpus Christi 2005, no pet.)

- Issue: *Rule 3.08 — Lawyer as witness*
- Disqualified

In re Gerry, 173 S.W.3d 901 (Tex. App.—Tyler 2005, no pet.)

- Issue: *Rule 1.05 — Confidentiality of information; Rule 1.09 — Former-client conflict of interest*
- Disqualified *(substitution denied)*

City of Dallas v. Redbird Dev. Corp., 143 S.W.3d 375 (Tex. App.—Dallas 2004, no pet.)

- Issues: *Rule 1.06 — Concurrent conflict of interest; Rule 1.09 — Former-client conflict of interest*
- No disqualification

In re Southwestern Bell Yellow Pages, Inc., 141 S.W.3d 229 (Tex. App.—San Antonio 2004, orig. proceeding)

- Issue: *Rule 1.06 — Concurrent conflict of interest*
- No disqualification

In re Barnes, 2003 WL 1848763 (Tex. App.—Beaumont 2003, orig. proceeding)

- Issue: *Rule 1.09 — Former-client conflict of interest*
- No disqualification

Lehmberg v. Lehmberg, 2003 WL 1964183 (Tex. App.—San Antonio 2003, no pet.)

- Issue: *Waiver of disqualification*
- No disqualification

Pollard v. Merkel, 114 S.W.3d 695 (Tex. App.—Dallas 2003, no pet.)

- Issue: *Rule 1.05 — Confidentiality of Information;*

Rule 1.09 — Former-client conflict of interest
- Disqualified

In re Skiles, 102 S.W.3d 323 (Tex. App.—Beaumont 2003, orig. proceeding)
- Issue: *Duty to preserve confidences of a non-client (or joint defense privilege)*
- Disqualified

Aghili v. Banks, 63 S.W.3d 812 (Tex. App.—Houston [14th Dist.] 2002, pet. denied)
- Issue: *Rule 3.08 — Lawyer as witness*
- Disqualified

In re Atherton, 2002 WL 31160059 (Tex. App.—Dallas 2002, orig. proceeding)
- Issue: *Rule 3.08 — Lawyer as witness*
- No disqualification

COC Servs., Ltd. v. CompUSA, Inc., 2002 WL 1792479 (Tex. App.—Dallas 2002, no pet.)
- Issue: *Rule 1.09 — Former-client conflict of interest*
- No disqualification

In re McCormick, 2002 WL 31076557 (Tex. App.—Tyler 2002, orig. proceeding)
- Issue: *Rule 1.06 — Concurrent conflict of interest (multiple clients); Rule 3.08 — Lawyer as witness*
- No disqualification

In re Robinson, 90 S.W.3d 921 (Tex. App.—San Antonio 2002, orig. proceeding)
- Issue: *Standing; Rule 1.06 — Concurrent conflict of interest*
- No disqualification

In re Taylor, 67 S.W.3d 530 (Tex. App.—Waco 2002, orig. proceeding)

- Issue: *Rule 1.06 — Concurrent conflict of interest; Waiver of disqualification*
- Disqualified

In re Posadas USA, Inc., 100 S.W.3d 254 (Tex. App.—San Antonio 2001, no pet.)

- Issue: *Rule 1.06 — Concurrent conflict of interest*
- *Withdrawal of attorney, mandamus granted*

In re Roseland Oil & Gas, Inc., 68 S.W.3d 784 (Tex. App.— Eastland 2001, orig. proceeding)

- Issue: *Rule 1.09 — Former-client conflict of interest*
- Disqualified

In re Bahn, 13 S.W.3d 865 (Tex. App.—Fort Worth 2000, orig. proceeding)

- Issue: *Rule 3.08 — Lawyer as witness*
- *Attorney 1* disqualified *(for trial, not pre-trial);* No disqualification of *co-counsel*

In re Cap Rock Elec. Coop., 35 S.W.3d 222 (Tex. App.—Texarkana 2000, orig. proceeding)

- Issue: *Rule 1.09 — Former-client conflict of interest*
- No disqualification

In re Chonody, 49 S.W.3d 376 (Tex. App.—Fort Worth 2000, orig. proceeding)

- Issue: *Rule 1.09 — Former-client conflict of interest*
- No disqualification

Jones v. Lurie, 32 S.W.3d 737 (Tex. App.—Houston [14th Dist.] 2000, no pet.)

- Issue: *Rule 1.09 — Former-client conflict of*

interest; Waiver of disqualification; Standing
- No disqualification

Massey v. Columbus State Bank, 35 S.W.3d 697 (Tex. App.—Houston [1st Dist.] 2000, pet. denied)
- Issue: *Waiver of disqualification*
- No disqualification

In re Rubin, 23 S.W.3d 382 (Tex. App.—Amarillo 2000, orig. proceeding [mand. denied])
- Issue: *Disqualification for non-lawyer conflict*
- No disqualification

Cruz v. Hinojosa, 12 S.W.3d 545 (Tex. App.—San Antonio 1999, pet. denied)
- Issue: *Rule 1.09 — Former-client conflict of interest*
- No disqualification

In re A.M., 974 S.W.2d 857 (Tex. App.—San Antonio 1998, no pet.)
- Issues: Rule 3.08 — Lawyer as witness; Disqualification as a sanction for misconduct
- No disqualification

Ghidoni v. Stone Oak, Inc., 966 S.W.2d 573 (Tex. App.—San Antonio 1998, pet. denied)
- Issue: *Rule 1.09 — Former-client conflict of interest*
- No disqualification

In re Acevedo, 956 S.W.2d 770 (Tex. App.—San Antonio 1997, orig. proceeding)
- Issue: *Rule 3.08 — Lawyer as witness*
- No disqualification

Arteaga v. Texas Dep't of Protective & Regulatory Servs., 924 S.W.2d 756 (Tex. App.—Austin 1996, writ denied)

- Issue: *Rule 1.09 — Former client conflict of interest*
- No disqualification

Arzate v. Hayes, 915 S.W.2d 616 (Tex. App.—El Paso 1996, writ dism'd)

- Issue: *Rule 1.06 — Concurrent conflict of interest*
- No disqualification

Schwartz v. Jefferson, 930 S.W.2d 957 (Tex. App.—Houston [14th Dist.] 1996, orig. proceeding)

- Issue: *Rule 3.08 — Lawyer as witness*
- No disqualification

Smirl v. Bridewell, 932 S.W.2d 743 (Tex. App.—Waco 1996, orig. proceeding [leave denied])

- Issue: *Rule 1.06 — concurrent conflict of interest*
- No disqualification

Spain v. Montalvo, 921 S.W.2d 852 (Tex. App.—San Antonio 1996, orig. proceeding [leave denied])

- Issue: *Rule 3.08 — Lawyers as witness*
- Disqualified for trial, but allowed to help in preparation

Centerline Indus., Inc. v. Knize, 894 S.W.2d 874 (Tex. App.—Waco 1995, orig. proceeding)

- Issue: *Rule 1.09 — Former-client conflict of interest*
- Disqualified

Rio Hondo Implement Co. v. Euresti, 903 S.W.2d 128 (Tex. App.—Corpus Christi 1995, orig. proceeding [mand. denied])

- Issue: *Waiver of disqualification; Duty to preserve confidences of a non-client (joint defense privilege)*

- No disqualification

Wasserman v. Black, 910 S.W.2d 564 (Tex. App.—Waco 1995, orig. proceeding)
- Issue: *Rule 1.09 — Former-client conflict of interest; Waiver of disqualification*
- Disqualified

May v. Crofts, 868 S.W.2d 397 (Tex. App.—Texarkana 1993, orig. proceeding)
- Issue: *Rule 3.08 — Lawyer as witness*
- No disqualification

Davis v. Stansbury, 824 S.W. 2d 278 (Tex. App.—Houston [1st Dist.] 1992, orig. proceeding)
- Issues: *Rule 1.05 - Confidentiality of information; Rule 1.06 — Concurrent conflict of interest; Rule 1.09 — Former-client conflict of interest*
- No disqualification

Haley v. Boles, 824 S.W.2d 796 (Tex. App.—Tyler 1992, orig. proceeding)
- Issue: *Rule 1.06 — Concurrent conflict of interest; 6th Amendment Right to Conflict-Free Representation*
- Withdrawal of attorney, mandamus relief granted

HECI Exploration Co. v. Clajon Gas Co., 843 S.W.2d 622 (Tex. App.—Austin 1992, writ denied)
- Issue: *Rule 1.09 — Former-client conflict of interest; Waiver of disqualification*
- No disqualification

Clarke v. Ruffino, 819 S.W. 2d 947 (Tex. App.—Houston [14th Dist.] 1991, orig. proceeding)
- Issues: *Rule 1.05 — Disclosure of confidential*

> *information; Rule 1.06 — Concurrent conflict of*
> *interest; Rule 1.09 — Former-client conflict of*
> *interest*
> * Disqualified

Conoco Inc. v. Baskin, 803 S.W.2d 416 (Tex. App.—El Paso 1991, no writ)

* Issue: *Rule 1.06 — Concurrent conflict of interest*
* No disqualification

Schwager v. Texas Commerce Bank, N.A., 813 S.W.2d 225 (Tex. App.—Houston [1st Dist.] 1991, no writ)

* Issue: *Rule 3.08 — Lawyer as witness*
* No disqualification

Home Ins. Co. v. Marsh, 790 S.W.2d 749 (Tex. App.—El Paso 1990, orig. proceeding [leave denied])

* Issue: *Rule 1.09 — Former-client conflict of interest*
* Disqualified

Howard v. Texas Dept. of Human Servs., 791 S.W.2d 313 (Tex. App.—Corpus Christi 1990, no writ)

* Issue: *Rule 1.09 — Former-client conflict of interest*
* Disqualified

Insurance Co. of N. Am. v. Westergren, 794 S.W.2d 812 (Tex. App.—Corpus Christi 1990, orig. proceeding [leave denied])

* Issue: *Rule 1.09 — Former-client conflict of*
  interest and disqualification of law firm; Waiver of
  disqualification
* Disqualified

Samuels v. Montgomery, 793 S.W.2d 337 (Tex. App.—Houston [14th Dist.] 1990, orig. proceeding [leave denied])

* Issue: *Rule 1.09 — Former-client conflict of interest*
  (lawyer hired by new firm, which is the opposing

counsel of a case she previously worked on, but is not working at the new firm yet)
- No disqualification

Petroleum Wholesale, Inc. v. Marshall, 751 S.W.2d 295 (Tex. App.—Dallas 1988, no writ)
- Issue: *Disciplinary Rule 4-101(B), Canon 4 Presumption of Shared Confidences and TCPR Canon 9 Appearance of Impropriety, counterpart Rule 1.09 — Former-client conflict of interest, disqualification of law firm*
- Disqualified

5th Circuit Court of Appeals cases

In re Proeducation Intl., Inc., 587 F.3d 296 (5th Cir. 2009)
- Issue: *Rule 1.09 — Former-client conflict of interest, imputed knowledge*
- No disqualification

United States v. Gharbi, 510 F.3d 550 (5th Cir. 2007)
- Issue: *6th Amendment Right to Conflict-Free Representation*
- Disqualified

FDIC v. U.S. Fire Ins. Co., 50 F.3d 1304 (5th Cir. 1995)
- Issues: *Rule 3.08 — Lawyer as witness; Appearance of impropriety*
- Disqualified *two attorneys,* no disqualification of *law firm*

Forsyth v. Barr, 19 F.3d 1527 (5th Cir. 1994)
- Issue: *Rule 1.06 — Concurrent conflict of interest*
- Disqualified

Resolution Trust Corp. v. Bright, 6 F.3d 336 (5th Cir. 1993)

- Issue: *Rule 3.04(b) — Fairness in adjudicatory proceedings; 4.01(a) — Truthfulness in statements to others; 4.04(a) — Respect for rights of third persons (all in regards to conduct during interview of a witness)*
- No disqualification

In re American Airlines Inc., 972 F.2d 605 (5th Cir. 1992), *cert denied*, 113 S.Ct. 1262 (1993)

- Issues: *Rule 1.06 — Concurrent conflict of interest; Rule 1.09 - Former-client conflict of interest*
- Disqualified

In re Dresser Indus. Inc., 972 F.2d 540 (5th Cir. 1992)

- Issue: *Rule 1.06 — Concurrent conflict of interest*
- Disqualified

Musicus v. Westinghouse Elec. Corp., 621 F.2d 742 (5th Cir. 1980)

- Issue: *Rule 1.09 — Former-client conflict of interest*
- *Vacated and remanded*

Wilson P. Abraham Constr. Corp. v. Armco Steel Corp., 559 F.2d 250 (5th Cir. 1977)

- Issue: *Duty to preserve confidences of a non-client (or joint defense privilege)*
- *Remanded for further consideration*

In re Gopman, 531 F.2d 262 (5th Cir. 1976)

- Issue: *Rule 1.06 — Concurrent conflict of interest*
- Disqualified

Woods v. Covington County Bank, 537 F.2d 804 (5th Cir. 1976)

- Issue: *Canon 9 Appearance of Impropriety, counterpart Rule 1.10 - successive government &*

private employment
- No disqualification

In re Yarn Processing Patent Validity Litigation, 530 F.2d 83 (5th Cir. 1976)
- Issue: *Standing*
- No disqualification

American Can Co. v. Citrus Feed Co., 436 F.2d 1125 (5th Cir. 1971)
- Issue: *Canon 6 — Conflicting interests, counterpart Rule 1.09 - Former-client conflict of interest; Canon 37 — Client Confidences, counterpart Rule 1.05 - Confidentiality of information*
- No disqualification

Other Federal court cases

Coates v. Brazoria County, 2012 WL 2568129 (S.D. Tex. 2012)
- Issue: *Rule 1.09 Former-client conflict of interest; Standing*
- No disqualification

John Crane Production Solutions, Inc. v. R2R and D, LLC, 2012 WL 3453696 (N.D. Tex. 2012)
- Issue: *Rule 1.09 — Former-client conflict of interest*
- Disqualified

Randall v. BAC Home Loans Servicing, LP, 2012 WL 1899553 (E.D. Tex. 2012)
- Issue: *Rule 3.08 — Lawyer as witness*
- No disqualification

United States v. Precision Impact Recovery LLC, 2011 WL 609902 (N.D. Tex. 2011)
- Issue: *Rule 1.09 — Former-client conflict of interest*

- Disqualified

Classic Ink, Inc. v. Rowdies, 2010 WL 2927285 (N.D. Tex. 2010)
- Issue: *Rule 1.09 — Former-client conflict of interest; Rule 3.08 — Lawyer as witness (in a footnote)*
- No disqualification

JuxtaComm-Texas Software, LLC v. Axway, Inc., 2010 WL 4920909 (E.D. Tex. 2010)
- Issue: ABA Model Rule 1.07, counterpart *Rule 1.09 — Former-client conflict of interest*
- No disqualification

Soverain Software LLC v. CDW Corp., 2010 WL 1038731 (E.D. Tex. 2010)
- Issue: *Rule 1.09 — Former-client conflict of interest*
- No disqualification

United States v. Pineda, 2010 WL 5510136 (E.D. Tex. 2010)
- Issue: *6th Amendment Right to Conflict-Free Representation; Rule 1.09 — Former-client conflict of interest; Rule 3.08 — Lawyer as witness*
- Disqualified

Vinewood Capital LLC v. Dar Al-Maal Al-Islami Trust, 2010 WL 1172947 (N.D. Tex. 2010)
- Issue: *Rule 1.09 — Former-client conflict of interest; Waiver of disqualification*
- No disqualification

Vinewood Capital, LLC v. Sheppard Mullin Richter & Hampton, LLP, 2010 WL 3283043 (N.D. Tex. 2010)
- Issue: *Rule 1.09 — Former-client conflict of interest; Waiver of disqualification*
- No disqualification

Clemens v. McNamee, 2008 WL 1969315 (S.D. Tex. 2008)
- Issue: *Rule 1.09 — Former-client conflict of interest*
- No disqualification

Hill v. Hunt, 2008 WL 4108120 (N.D. Tex. 2008)
- Issue: ABA Model Rule 1.07, counterpart *Rule 1.06 — Concurrent conflict of interest*
- Disqualified

Marin v. Gilberg, 2008 WL 2770382 (S.D. Tex. 2008)
- Issue: *Rule 3.08 — Lawyer as witness*
- Attorney disqualified, no disqualification of law firm

Biax Corp. v. Fujitsu Computer Systs. Corp., 2007 WL 1466638 (E.D. Tex. 2007)
- Issue: *Rule 1.09 — Former-client conflict of interest*
- No disqualification

Calhoun v. City of Austin, 2007 WL 496721 (W.D. Tex. 2007)
- Issue: *Rule 3.08 — Lawyer as witness*
- No disqualification

Landmark Graphics Corp. v. Seismic Micro Technology, Inc., 2007 WL 735007 (S.D. Tex. 2007)
- Issue: *Rule 3.08 — Lawyer as witness*
- No disqualification

Mendoza v. United States, 481 F. Supp. 2d 650 (W.D. Tex. 2007)
- Issue: *Rule 3.08 — Lawyer as witness*
- No disqualification, attorney's affidavit inadmissible

Microsoft Corp. v. Commonwealth Scientific & Industrial Research Org., 2007 WL 4376104 (E.D. Tex. 2007)
- Issue: ABA Model Rule 1.07, counterparts *Rule 1.06 — Concurrent conflict of interest and*

> *Rule 1.09 — Former-client conflict of interest;*
> *Disqualification for receipt of confidential*
> *information; Waiver of disqualification*
> * No disqualification

Crossroad Systs. (Texas), Inc. v. Dot Hill Systs. Corp., 2006 WL 1544621 (W.D. Tex. 2006)

* Issue: *Rule 3.08 — Lawyer as witness*
* Disqualified

Grosser-Samuels v. Jacquelin Designs Enters., Inc., 448 F. Supp. 2d 772 (N.D. Tex. 2006)

* Issue: *Rule 1.06 — Concurrent conflict of interest;*
  Rule 1.09 — Former-client conflict of interest
  and co-counsel disqualification; Appearance of
  impropriety
* Disqualified

Sourceprose Corp. v. Fidelity Nat'l Fin., 2006 WL 887394 (E.D. Tex. 2006)

* Issue: *Rule 1.09 — Former-client conflict of interest,*
  disqualification of law firm
* Likely disqualified (defendants given time to provide evidence)

United States v. Aleman, 2004 WL 1834602 (W.D. Tex. 2004)

* Issue: *6th Amendment Right to Conflict-Free*
  Representation; Rule 1.09 — Former-client conflict
  of interest
* No disqualification

Great Am. Ins. Co. v. Christopher, 2003 WL 21414676 (N.D. Tex. 2003)

* Issue: *Rule 1.05 — Confidentiality of information;*
  Rule 1.09 — Former-client conflict of interest
* No disqualification

160

United States v. Burraston, 178 F. Supp.2d 730 (W.D. Tex. 2002)
- Issue: *6th Amendment Right to Conflict-Free Representation*
- No disqualification, deposition suppressed

Advanced Display Sys., Inc. v. Kent State Univ., 2001 WL 1524433 (N.D. Tex. 2001)
- Issue: *Rule 1.06 — Concurrent conflict of interest*
- No disqualification

Cramer v. Sabine Transp. Co., 141 F. Supp.2d 727 (S.D. Tex. 2001)
- Issue: *Texas Rule 4.02 — Anti-contact*
- No disqualification

Islander E. Rental Program v. Ferguson, 917 F. Supp. 504 (S.D. Tex. 1996)
- Issue: *Rule 1.09 — Former-client conflict of interest; Waiver of disqualification*
- Disqualified

Turner v. Firestone Tire & Rubber Co., 896 F. Supp. 651 (E.D. Tex. 1995)
- Issue: *Rule 1.06 — Concurrent conflict of interest; Rule 1.09 — Former-client conflict of interest; Waiver of disqualification; Duty to preserve confidences of a non-client (or joint defense privilege)*
- No disqualification

Carbo Ceramics Inc. v. Norton-Alcoa Proppants, 155 F.R.D. 158 (N.D. Tex. 1994)
- Issue: *Rule 1.09 — Former-client conflict of interest*
- No disqualification

Lelsz v. Kavanagh, 137 F.R.D. 646 (N.D. Tex. 1991)

- Issue: *Disqualification as a sanction*
- Disqualified

Shelton v. Hess, 599 F. Supp. 905 (S.D. Tex. 1984)

- Issue: *TCPR Canon 7 Communication with Adverse Interest (plaintiff's attorney met with one of the defendants without consulting opposing counsel); Canon 9 Appearance of Impropriety*
- Disqualified

Chapter 21

PEC Opinions Addressing Principal Conflict of Interest Rules

Listed below by are the Opinions of the Texas Supreme Court's Professional Ethics Committee that address the principal Texas Disciplinary Rules of Professional Conduct concerning conflicts of interest: Rules 1.06, 1.07, 1.08, 1.09, 1.10, and 1.11.

The State Bar Act, as amended in 1987, created the Professional Ethics Committee.[1] The Texas Supreme Court appoints the nine-member committee, and members serve three-year terms.[2] On request of a member of the State Bar, or on its own initiative, the Committee "express[es] its opinion on the propriety of professional conduct other than on a question pending before a court of this state."[3] The statute expressly provides that the Committee's opinions are not binding on the Texas Supreme Court,[4] and Texas courts have generally held that the Opinions are advisory, not binding.[5] Thus, some court decisions have not followed the Committee's Opinions in particular fact settings.[6]

---

[1] *See* Tex. Gov't Code §§ 81.091-.095.

[2] *Id.* § 81.091(a).

[3] *Id.* § 81.092(a).

[4] *Id.* § 81.092(c).

[5] *See generally Royston, Rayzor, Vickery, & Williams, LLP v. Lopez*, 467 S.W.3d 494, 503 (Tex. 2015) ("Opinions of the Professional Ethics Committee carry less weight than do the Disciplinary Rules as to legal obligations of attorneys, but they are nevertheless advisory as to those obligations. . . . Without addressing or diminishing to any degree the ethical obligations of attorneys, we are mindful that the parties to an agreement determine its terms, and courts must respect those terms as 'sacred', absent compelling reasons to do otherwise.").

[6] *See Gray v. Noteboom*, 159 S.W.3d 750, 752-53 (Tex. App.—Fort Worth 2005, pet. denied) ("[O]pinion 459 of the Texas Professional Ethics Committee . . . states it is not proper for a law firm to have an employment agreement or partnership agreement which provides that upon leaving the

PEC Opinions Concerning Rule 1.06

Op. 650, 2015 WL 3602350 (6/15) — a law firm hiring a marketing assistant who was employed by a firm that currently represents the defendant in a lawsuit in which the hiring firm represents the plaintiff

Op. 649, 2015 WL 3948510 (5/15) — representing a federal agency against employment furlough claims, when the lawyer representing the agency may have a similar claim against the agency in the future

Op. 645, 2014 WL 5149942 (10/14) — representing a debtor in a bankruptcy case in which the lawyer also represents a creditor in unrelated matters or the creditor is a former client

Op. 644, 2014 WL 4960462 (8/14) — a law firm hiring a new lawyer who, before becoming a lawyer, was a law clerk in the firm that represents the opposing party in the current lawsuit

Op. 643, 2014 WL 3038026 (5/14) — a lawyer arranging for a debt-management services company owned by the lawyer to refer company customers to the lawyer's firm on matters unre-

---

firm, the associate or the partner would be required to pay his former law firm a percentage of fees thereafter from clients brought from his former law firm. Appellant contends this rule [5.06] and opinion were violated in the partnership agreement and their enforcement by the award of the arbitration panel . . . . In the instant case, there appears to be no question about the fact that the partnership agreement is contrary to the Ethics Committee opinion . . . . It appears the ethics opinion, in an effort to be fair to the withdrawing attorney, is not mindful of the rights of the firm or attorney remaining. We hold that a violation of opinion 459 of the Texas Professional Ethics Committee, under the circumstances of this case, is not contrary to public policy and should not be used as a procedural weapon."); *Stonewall Financial Services Corp. v. Corona*, 2012 WL 4087642, at *3 (Tex. App.—Texarkana 2012, no pet.) ("Because the rulings of the Committee on Professional Ethics are binding on neither the trial court nor on us, we do not find any situation which would have deprived the trial court of jurisdiction.").

lated to matters on which the company services the customers

Op. 641, 2014 WL 2510793 (5/14) — a lawyer accepting client referrals from a financial-planning services company that regularly retains the lawyer for matters unrelated to the matters involved in the client referrals, versus accepting referrals of customers in matters involving financial or investment issues or the customer's relationship with the company

Op. 637, 2013 WL 5508575 (8/13) — including in a lawyer-client agreement a waiver of barratry claims against the lawyer; negotiating settlement of a client's civil-barratry claim

Op. 635, 2013 WL 5508570 (8/13) — advising, for a fee, a pro se litigant in a family-law matter concerning "self-help" forms prepared by the litigant if the lawyer conditions the advice on the client's agreement that no lawyer-client relationship exists; providing services to the other spouse in the case

Op. 633, 2013 WL 4791439 (7/13) — a lawyer-employee of a city that jointly owns an entity with another city acting as general counsel of the entity

Op. 624, 2013 WL 1776543 (2/13) — including in a lawyer-client engagement agreement for representing a misdemeanor-case client a provision in which the client gives advance authority for the lawyer to enter a plea of "no contest" or "guilty" in the case; acting as the client's bail bondsman

Op. 615, 2012 WL 2168702 (4/12) — a district attorney investigating and prosecuting a local elected official in a criminal proceeding or civil-removal proceeding when the district attorney previously represented the official on matters relating to the official's performance of public duties

Op. 608, 2011 WL 5831796 (8/11) — a lawyer with a legal-services entity representing a child in a custody matter against a former client whom another lawyer with the legal-services entity represented in an unrelated matter

Op. 599, 2010 WL 3479017 (7/10) — a lawyer who serves as bail bondsman and criminal defense lawyer for a client; entering into an agreement with the client that authorizes the lawyer, if the client fails to appear in court, to enter a "no contest" plea that will have the effect of a guilty plea

Op. 593, 2010 WL 1026287 (2/10) — entering into an agreement with a client, who is not represented by independent counsel, for the settlement of the client's malpractice claim against the lawyer for failing to file the client's lawsuit before the limitations period expired

Op. 583, 2008 WL 4897790 (9/08) — agreeing to serve as both a mediator between parties in a divorce and as a lawyer to the parties to prepare the divorce decree and other documents necessary to effect the agreement resulting from mediation

Op. 581, 2008 WL 4535053 (4/08) — including in a litigation engagement agreement a provision that requires the client to pay defense expenses incurred by the lawyer if the lawyer is later joined as a defendant in the litigation

Op. 579, 2007 WL 4916954 (11/07) — a lawyer in a public defender's office avoiding a conflict related to the representation of two defendants against criminal charges arising from the same incident by either referring one defendant to another lawyer in the same public defender's office or withdrawing from the representation of one defendant and continuing to represent the other

Op. 575, 2006 WL 4045664 (11/06) — a lawyer recording his telephone conversations with a client or third party without first informing the client or third party that the conversation is being recorded

Op. 571, 2006 WL 2038683 (5/06) — advising a criminal defendant about a plea agreement that would waive post-conviction appeals based on claims that the lawyer rendered ineffective assistance of counsel

Op. 569, 2006 WL 2038681 (4/06) — providing legal representation to a client in a matter against a third party who was a customer of a business owned by the lawyer that provides law-related consulting services and represents to its customers that it will not share their confidential information

Op. 567, 2006 WL 1148498 (2/06) — a lawyer in private practice providing legal advice to a city ethics board concerning an ethics complaint against a majority of the members of the city council while the lawyer simultaneously serves as the city attorney at the discretion of the city council with compensation set by the city council

Op. 565, 2006 WL 1148496 (1/06) — representing a client in an appeal after the client filed grievances against the lawyer based on the lawyer's actions in part of the underlying litigation unrelated to the appeal

Op. 564, 2005 WL 3782936 (10/05) — representing a school district in its purchase of real estate from an individual who is a member of the board of directors of a bank that the lawyer's firm represents in unrelated matters

Op. 563, 2005 WL 3689003 (10/05) — soliciting and accepting employment from a client on a contingent-fee basis after leaving a firm that represented the client in the same matter on an hourly basis

Op. 560, 2005 WL 2755022 (8/05) — a law firm leasing lawyers and non-lawyer personnel from an employee leasing company that also leases lawyers and non-lawyer personnel to other firms

Op. 557, 2005 WL 5368333 (5/05) — a lawyer continuing to represent a client after the client tells the lawyer that the client consulted with a malpractice lawyer regarding the representation

Op. 555, 2004 WL 3176889 (12/04) — entering into a business arrangement with a chiropractor that involves the lawyer's referring clients to the chiropractor while owning a portion of the chiropractor's office and sharing in its profits

Op. 554, 2004 WL 2505504 (8/04) — a lawyer who is a state representative or state senator representing clients in a city, county, or state court in the lawyer's legislative district

Op. 547, 2001 WL 1202315 (1/03) — a law firm entering into an informal arrangement with a group of medical providers under which the group would pay for the firm's television advertising with the expectation (but not obligation) that the firm would refer its new clients to the medical group if they needed medical services

Op. 543, 2002 WL 1619398 (4/02) — a lawyer who is employed as in-house counsel for a healthcare provider and also maintains a separate law firm, entering into an agreement for the firm to provide low-cost legal services to the healthcare provider's patients

Op. 541, 2002 WL 405092 (2/02) — a municipal court judge representing a criminal defendant in a matter in which he has not acted in a judicial capacity but in which the city's police might be witnesses

Op. 540, 2002 WL 405091 (2/02) — a lawyer who is a county judge, and any lawyer in the private law firm with which the judge practices, representing private clients in the justice of the peace courts, statutory county courts, and district courts of the county in which the lawyer serves as judge

Op. 539, 2002 WL 405090 (2/02) — representing defendants in criminal cases in the county in which the lawyer's spouse is an assistant district attorney

Op. 538, 2001 WL 1042230 (6/01) — a lawyer who is a newly elected district attorney prosecuting a former client in a new criminal proceeding or in a probation revocation proceeding in a case in which the lawyer served as defense counsel in the original proceeding

Op. 537, 2001 WL 557899 (5/01) — a lawyer who is the general counsel of a trade association recommending outside counsel, at the request of association members, to represent the members in potential litigation against a common supplier

Op. 536, 2001 WL 557898 (5/01) — receiving solicitation fees from an investment adviser for referring the lawyer's clients to the investment adviser

Op. 535, 2000 WL (9/00) — participating in a court-sponsored program involving the provision of limited legal services to criminal defendants when the county pays a fee to the lawyer only if the defendant agrees to plead guilty

Op. 533, 2000 WL 987291 (1/00) — a lawyer who is retained by an insurance company to defend its policyholders agreeing to comply with restrictions imposed by the insurance company to limit the manner in which the lawyer defends the policyholders

Op. 531, 1999 WL 1007267 (1/99) — simultaneously representing a corporation and its subsidiaries

Op. 530, 1999 WL (10/99) — a lawyer who is a county commissioner, and any member of the lawyer's firm, practicing in the justice, statutory county, and district courts of the county in which the lawyer serves as a commissioner

Op. 528, 1998 WL 1064546 (12/98) — a law firm hiring a lawyer who is married to a mid-level employee of a corporation that is the defendant in an ongoing lawsuit in which the firm represents the plaintiffs

Op. 527, 1998 WL 749173 (10/98) — a law firm composed of former members of another law firm representing a party in litigation in which the former firm represents the opposing party

Op. 525, 1998 WL 130065 (3/98) — a lender's lawyer preparing, at the borrower's expense, loan documents or a deed related to a residential loan

Op. 519, 1997 WL 16662 (3/97) — a law firm that represents a foreign government administering and controlling a legal aid office established by the foreign government to provide legal services to its nationals who reside in Texas

Op. 515, 1996 WL 277337 (7/96) — entering into an arrangement with a contract-lawyer placement agency under which the agency will seek to place the lawyer with law firms and corporate legal departments for work on short-term legal projects

Op. 512, 1995 WL 374884 (12/95) — a corporation's in-house lawyer representing a joint venture in which the corporation is a venturer

Op. 511, 1995 WL 248471 (1/95) — a law firm representing two children in a civil action concerning an auto accident in which their mother was killed and their father, whom the law firm represents, was involved and is a possible defendant

Op. 508, 1995 WL 908218 (9/95) — a law firm leasing its employees, including its lawyers, from a leasing company (owned by non-lawyers) that also leases employees, including lawyers, to other law firms

Op. 501, 1995 WL 908210 (5/95) — representing a husband in a divorce action after the wife consulted with the lawyer's former law partner concerning the divorce but did not actually hire the former partner when she later filed for divorce

Op. 500, 1995 WL 913236 (4/95) — representing both the driver and a passenger in a personal injury case arising from a collision or representing two people injured in a single accident

Op. 497, 1994 WL 417012 (11/94) — a lawyer who is a city commissioner representing criminal defendants in cases in which (1) the city police department participates in the defendant's arrest or the criminal investigation, (2) members of the city police department are victims, or (3) the city judge issues an arrest or search warrant

Op. 494, 1994 WL 65262 (7/94) — representing a wife in a divorce action six years after a brief consultation with the husband regarding a possible divorce action that the husband never filed

Op. 487, 1994 WL 911696 (3/94) — representing an employer and employee who are defendants in an employment lawsuit filed by a former employee

Op. 483, 1994 WL 848490 (2/94) — referring clients to companies in which the lawyer has an ownership interest

Op. 476, 1992 WL 315148 (10/92) — a lawyer, who is employed by an organization to assist its members, deciding whether to refer the members to outside counsel in a situation in which outside counsel are paid under an insurance policy funded by members' dues

Op. 472, 1992 WL 792969 (5/92) — hiring a secretary or legal assistant who was fired by a law firm during the pendency of a lawsuit in which the hiring firm and the firing firm are opposing counsel

Op. 465, 1991 WL 425385 (1/91) — owning an interest in a lending institution that loans money to the lawyer's personal injury clients or borrowing money from a lending institution for a personal injury client's case expenses and passing on the interest and finance charges to the client

PEC Opinions Concerning Rule 1.07

Op. 583, 2008 WL 4897790 (9/08) — serving both as a mediator between parties in a divorce and as a lawyer to prepare the divorce decree and other necessary legal documents resulting from the mediation

Op. 512, 1995 WL 374884 (12/95) — an in-house lawyer simultaneously representing both a corporation and a joint venture entity in which the corporation is a venturer

PEC Opinions Concerning Rule 1.08

Op. 637, 2013 WL 550875 (8/13) — including in a lawyer-client agreement a waiver of barratry claims against the lawyer; negotiating settlement of a client's civil-barratry claim

Op. 633, 2013 WL 4791439 (7/13) — a lawyer employee of a city that jointly owns an entity with another city acting as general counsel of the entity

Op. 624, 2013 WL 1776543 (2/13) — acting as the client's bail bondsman

Op. 610, 2011 WL 5831798 (8/11) — entering into a contingent-fee agreement with a client under which the client grants to the lawyer a security interest in the litigation that is the subject of the representation, as a means of securing payment of the lawyer's fee

Op. 599, 2010 WL 3479017 (7/10) — a lawyer serving as bail bondsman for his criminal client including in the court's form of bond a provision in which the client agrees that, if the client fails to appear in court, the attorney may enter a "no contest" plea

Op. 596, 2010 WL 2480776 (4/10) — accepting an assignment of proceeds of an insurance policy as compensation for legal services

Op. 593, 2010 WL 1026287 (2/10) — settling a malpractice claim with a client not represented by independent counsel

Op. 586, 2008 WL 5680298 (10/08) — including a binding arbitration provision in attorney-client engagement agreements

Op. 581, 2008 WL 4535053 (4/08) — including a provision in an engagement agreement that requires the client to pay defense expenses incurred by the lawyer if the lawyer is later joined as a defendant in the litigation

Op. 571, 2006 WL 2038683 (5/06) — advising a criminal defendant on a plea agreement in which the defendant waives any post-conviction rights to appeal based on prosecutorial misconduct and ineffective assistance of counsel

Op. 566, 2006 WL 1148497 (2/06) — a lawyer who is acting as a receiver paying a portion of the receiver fees to lawyers representing the parties

Op. 542, 2002 WL 405093 (2/02) — entering into a fee arrangement with an insurance company in which the lawyer is compensated on a fixed fee basis for defined stages of representation in liability defense cases

Op. 483, 1994 WL 848490 (2/94) — jointly owning medical equipment with doctor when the equipment would be used to provide medical services to the lawyer's clients and the lawyer would share in profits earned by the use of the equipment

PEC Opinions Concerning Rule 1.09

Op. 650, 2015 WL 3602350 (6/15) — hiring a marketing assistant who was previously employed by a law firm that represents the defendant in a lawsuit in which the hiring firm represents the plaintiff

Op. 645, 2014 WL 5149942 (10/14) — representing a debtor in a bankruptcy case in which the creditor is a former client

Op. 644, 2014 WL 4960462 (8/14) — a law firm hiring a new lawyer who, before becoming a lawyer, was a law clerk in the firm that represents the opposing party in the current lawsuit

Op. 637, 2013 WL 5508575 (8/13) — including in a lawyer-client agreement a waiver of barratry claims against the lawyer; negotiating settlement of a client's civil-barratry claim

Op. 627, 2013 WL 2467807 (4/13) — disposing of the files of a former client after the lawyer who represented the client leaves the firm

Op. 615, 2012 WL 2168702 (4/12) — a district attorney investigating and prosecuting a local elected official in a criminal proceeding or civil-removal proceeding when the district attorney previously represented the official on matters relating to the official's performance of public duties

Op. 608, 2011 WL 5831796 (8/11) — a lawyer with a legal-services entity representing a child in a custody matter against a former client whom another legal-services lawyer represented in an unrelated matter

Op. 607, 2011 WL 5831795 (7/11) — a lawyer providing information concerning his prior legal work, including confidential information of former clients, to a new law firm that is considering the lawyer for employment

Op. 598, 2010 WL 3479016 (7/10) — a law firm continuing to represent a client in a lawsuit after the firm hires a lawyer who had previously represented the opposing party in another matter

Op. 584, 2008 WL 4897791 (9/08) — continuing to represent a client in a case after learning that the conduct of a former client might be material to the case

Op. 579, 2007 WL 4916954 (11/07) — a lawyer in a public defender's office avoiding a conflict related to the representation of two defendants against criminal charges arising from the same incident by either referring one defendant to another lawyer in the same public defender's office or withdrawing from the representation of one defendant and continuing to represent the other

Op. 578, 2007 WL 2954614 (7/07) — a law firm representing a municipality against another municipality that is a former client of the firm

Op. 538, 2001 WL 1042230 (6/01) — a lawyer who is a newly elected district attorney prosecuting a former client in a new criminal proceeding or in a probation revocation proceeding in a case in which the lawyer served as defense counsel in the original proceeding

Op. 527, 1998 WL 749173 (10/98) — a law firm composed of former members of another law firm representing a party in litigation in which the former firm represents the opposing party

Op. 519, 1997 WL 16662 (3/97) — a law firm that represents a foreign government administering and controlling a legal aid office established by the foreign government to provide legal services to its nationals who reside in Texas

Op. 515, 1996 WL 277337 (7/96) — entering into an arrangement with a contract lawyer placement agency under which the agency will seek to place the lawyer with law firms and corporate legal departments for work on short-term legal projects

Op. 501, 1995 WL 908210 (5/95) — representing a husband in a divorce action after the wife consulted with the lawyer's former law partner concerning the divorce but did not actually hire the former partner when she later filed for divorce

Op. 494, 1994 WL 65262 (7/94) — representing a wife in a divorce action six years after a brief consultation with the husband regarding a possible divorce action that the husband never filed

Op. 482, 1994 WL 848489 (2/94) — a law firm retained by an insurance company continuing to jointly defend an insured and its ex-employee after withdrawing from the representation of another ex-employee who provided confidential information to the law firm indicating that he would commit perjury unless he received a financial incentive from the insured

Op. 472, 1992 WL 792969 (5/92) — when two firms are opposing counsel in a lawsuit, and the one firm had fired a legal assistant and the other hired the legal assistant during the pendency of the lawsuit

PEC Opinions Concerning Rule 1.10

Op. 574, 2006 WL 3861338 (9/06) — former employee of a regulatory agency representing a client before the agency in a matter that originated during the lawyer's employment but in which the lawyer did not participate personally and substantially

Op. 551, 2004 WL 1590384 (5/04) — requiring a lawyer to comply with a provision of a city's ethics code that prohibits all former city employees from representing any unrelated person before the city for compensation for a period of two years after termination of employment with the city

Op. 544, 2002 WL 1619564 (4/02) — a lawyer participating in discussions and vote as a city council member on a matter involving a client of the lawyer's former law firm

Op. 538, 2001 WL 1042230 (6/01) — newly elected district attorney prosecuting clients who were his former clients in his previous position as state public defender

PEC Opinions Concerning Rule 1.11

Op. 583, 2008 WL 4897790 (8/08) — serving both as a mediator between parties in a divorce and as a lawyer to prepare the divorce decree and other necessary legal documents resulting from the mediation

Op. 541, 2002 WL 405092 (2/02) —a municipal court judge representing a criminal defendant in a matter in which the city's police may be potential witnesses

Op. 496, 1994 WL 417208 (11/94) — a law firm representing a client in action against a defendant when the lawyer in firm had previously acted as mediator in similar action involving defendant

APPENDIX

Texas Disciplinary Rules of Professional Conduct:

Key Rules for Disqualification

1.05 Confidentiality of Information

(a) "Confidential information" includes both "privileged information" and "unprivileged client information." "Privileged information" refers to the information of a client protected by the lawyer-client privilege of Rule 503 of the Texas Rules of Evidence or of Rule 503 of the Texas Rules of Criminal Evidence or by the principles of attorney-client privilege governed by Rule 501 of the Federal Rules of Evidence for United States Courts and Magistrates. "Unprivileged client information means" all information relating to a client or furnished by the client, other than privileged information, acquired by the lawyer during the course of or by reason of the representation of the client.

(b) Except as permitted by paragraphs (c) and (d), or as required by paragraphs (e), and (f), a lawyer shall not knowingly:

(1) Reveal confidential information of a client or a former client to:

(i) a person that the client has instructed is not to receive the information; or

(ii) anyone else, other than the client, the client's representatives, or the members, associates, or employees of the lawyer's law firm.

(2) Use confidential information of a client to the disadvantage of the client unless the client consents after consultations.

(3) Use confidential information of a former client to the disadvantage

of the former client after the representation is concluded unless the former client consents after consultation or the confidential information has become generally known.

(4) Use privileged information of a client for the advantage of the lawyer or of a third person, unless the client consents after consultation.

(c) A lawyer may reveal confidential information:

(1) When the lawyer has been expressly authorized to do so in order to carry out the representation.

(2) When the client consents after consultation.

(3) To the client, the client's representatives, or the members, associates, and employees of the lawyer's firm, except when otherwise instructed by the client.

(4) When the lawyer has reason to believe it is necessary to do so in order to comply with a court order, a Texas Disciplinary Rule of Professional Conduct, or other law.

(5) To the extent reasonably necessary to enforce a claim or establish a defense on behalf of the lawyer in a controversy between the lawyer and the client.

(6) To establish a defense to a criminal charge, civil claim or disciplinary complaint against the lawyer or the lawyer's associates based upon conduct involving the client or the representation of the client.

(7) When the lawyer has reason to believe it is necessary to do so in order to prevent the client from committing a criminal or fraudulent act.

(8) To the extent revelation reasonably appears necessary to rectify the consequences of a client's criminal or fraudulent act in the commission of which the lawyer's services had been used.

(d) A lawyer also may reveal unprivileged client information:

(1) When impliedly authorized to do so in order to carry out the representation.

(2) When the lawyer has reason to believe it is necessary to do so in order to:

(i) carry out the representation effectively;

(ii) defend the lawyer or the lawyer's employees or associates against a claim of wrongful conduct;

(iii) respond to allegations in any proceeding concerning the lawyer's representation of the client; or

(iv) prove the services rendered to a client, or the reasonable value thereof, or both, in an action against another person or organization responsible for the payment of the fee for services rendered to the client.

(e) When a lawyer has confidential information clearly establishing that a client is likely to commit a criminal or fraudulent act that is likely to result in death or substantial bodily harm to a person, the lawyer shall reveal confidential information to the extent revelation reasonably appears necessary to prevent the client from committing the criminal or fraudulent act.

(f) A lawyer shall reveal confidential information when required to do so by Rule 3.03(a)(2), 3.03(b), or by Rule 4.01(b).

Comment:

Confidentiality Generally

1. Both the fiduciary relationship existing between lawyer and client and the proper functioning of the legal system require the

preservation by the lawyer of confidential information of one who has employed or sought to employ the lawyer. Free discussion should prevail between lawyer and client in order for the lawyer to be fully informed and for the client to obtain the full benefit of the legal system. The ethical obligation of the lawyer to protect the confidential information of the client not only facilitates the proper representation of the client but also encourages potential clients to seek early legal assistance.

2. Subject to the mandatory disclosure requirements of paragraphs (e) and (f) the lawyer generally should be required to maintain confidentiality of information acquired by the lawyer during the course of or by reason of the representation of the client. This principle involves an ethical obligation not to use the information to the detriment of the client or for the benefit of the lawyer or a third person. In regard to an evaluation of a matter affecting a client for use by a third person, see Rule 2.02.

3. The principle of confidentiality is given effect not only in the Texas Disciplinary Rules of Professional Conduct but also in the law of evidence regarding the attorney-client privilege and in the law of agency. The attorney-client privilege, developed through many decades, provides the client a right to prevent certain confidential communications from being revealed by compulsion of law. Several sound exceptions to confidentiality have been developed in the evidence law of privilege. Exceptions exist in evidence law where the services of the lawyer were sought or used by a client in planning or committing a crime or fraud as well as where issues have arisen as to breach of duty by the lawyer or by the client to the other.

4. Rule 1.05 reinforces the principles of evidence law relating to the attorney-client privilege. Rule 1.05 also furnishes considerable protection to other information falling outside the scope of the privilege. Rule 1.05 extends ethical protection generally to unprivileged information relating to the client or furnished by the client during the course of or by reason of the representation of the client. In this respect Rule 1.05 accords with general fiduciary principles of agency.

5. The requirement of confidentiality applies to government lawyers

who may disagree with the policy goals that their representation is designed to advance.

Disclosure for Benefit of Client

6. A lawyer may be expressly authorized to make disclosures to carry out the representation and generally is recognized as having implied-in-fact authority to make disclosures about a client when appropriate in carrying out the representation to the extent that the client's instructions do not limit that authority. In litigation, for example, a lawyer may disclose information by admitting a fact that cannot properly be disputed, or in negotiation by making a disclosure that facilitates a satisfactory conclusion. The effect of Rule 1.05 is to require the lawyer to invoke, for the client, the attorney-client privilege when applicable; but if the court improperly denies the privilege, under paragraph (c)(4) the lawyer may testify as ordered by the court or may test the ruling as permitted by Rule 3.04(d).

7. In the course of a firm's practice, lawyers may disclose to each other and to appropriate employees information relating to a client, unless the client has instructed that particular information be confined to specified lawyers. Subparagraphs (b)(1) and (c)(3) continue these practices concerning disclosure of confidential information within the firm.

Use of Information

8. Following sound principles of agency law, subparagraphs (b)(2) and (4) subject a lawyer to discipline for using information relating to the representation in a manner disadvantageous to the client or beneficial to the lawyer or a third person, absent the informed consent of the client. The duty not to misuse client information continues after the client-lawyer relationship has terminated. Therefore, the lawyer is forbidden by subparagraph (b)(3) to use, in absence of the client's informed consent, confidential information of the former client to the client's disadvantage, unless the information is generally known.

Discretionary Disclosure Adverse to Client

9. In becoming privy to information about a client, a lawyer may foresee that the client intends serious and perhaps irreparable harm. To the extent a lawyer is prohibited from making disclosure, the interests of the potential victim are sacrificed in favor of preserving the client's information – usually unprivileged information – even though the client's purpose is wrongful. On the other hand, a client who knows or believes that a lawyer is required or permitted to disclose a client's wrongful purposes may be inhibited from revealing facts which would enable the lawyer to counsel effectively against wrongful action. Rule 1.05 thus involves balancing the interests of one group of potential victims against those of another. The criteria provided by the Rule are discussed below.

10. Rule 5.03 (d)(1) Texas Rules of Civil Evidence (Tex. R. Civ. Evid.), and Rule 5.03(d)(1), Texas Rules of Criminal Evidence (Tex. R. Crim. Evid.), indicate the underlying public policy of furnishing no protection to client information where the client seeks or uses the services of the lawyer to aid in the commission of a crime or fraud. That public policy governs the dictates of Rule 1.05. Where the client is planning or engaging in criminal or fraudulent conduct or where the culpability of the lawyer's conduct is involved, full protection of client information is not justified.

11. Several other situations must be distinguished. First, the lawyer may not counsel or assist a client in conduct that is criminal or fraudulent. See Rule 1.02(c). As noted in the Comment to that Rule, there can be situations where the lawyer may have to reveal information relating to the representation in order to avoid assisting a client's criminal or fraudulent conduct, and subparagraph (c)(4) permits doing so. A lawyer's duty under Rule 3.03(a) not to use false or fabricated evidence is a special instance of the duty prescribed in Rule 1.02(c) to avoid assisting a client in criminal or fraudulent conduct, and subparagraph (c)(4) permits revealing information necessary to comply with Rule 3.03(a) or (b). The same is true of compliance with Rule 4.01. See also paragraph (f).

12. Second, the lawyer may have been innocently involved in past conduct by the client that was criminal or fraudulent. In such a situation the lawyer has not violated Rule 1.02(c), because to "counsel or assist" criminal or fraudulent conduct requires knowing

that the conduct is of that character. Since the lawyer's services were made an instrument of the client's crime or fraud, the lawyer has a legitimate interest both in rectifying the consequences of such conduct and in avoiding charges that the lawyer's participation was culpable. Subparagraph (c)(6) and (8) give the lawyer professional discretion to reveal both unprivileged and privileged information in order to serve those interests. See paragraph (g). In view of Tex. R. Civ. Evid. Rule 5.03(d)(1), and Tex. R. Crim. Evid. 5.03(d)(1), however, rarely will such information be privileged.

13. Third, the lawyer may learn that a client intends prospective conduct that is criminal or fraudulent. The lawyer's knowledge of th client's purpose may enable the lawyer to prevent commission of the prospective crime or fraud. When the threatened injury is grave, the lawyer's interest in preventing the harm may be more compelling than the interest in preserving confidentiality of information. As stated in subparagraph (c)(7), the lawyer has professional discretion, based on reasonable appearances, to reveal both privileged and unprivileged information in order to prevent the client's commission of any criminal or fraudulent act. In some situations of this sort, disclosure is mandatory. See paragraph (e) and Comments 18-20.

14. The lawyer's exercise of discretion under paragraphs (c) and (d) involves consideration of such factors as the magnitude, proximity, and likelihood of the contemplated wrong, the nature of the lawyer's relationship with the client and with those who might be injured by the client, the lawyer's own involvement in the transaction, and factors that may extenuate the client's conduct in question. In any case a disclosure adverse to the client's interest should be no greater than the lawyer believes necessary to the purpose. Although preventive action is permitted by paragraphs (c) and (d), failure to take preventive action does not violate those paragraphs. But see paragraphs (e) and (f). Because these rules do not define standards of civil liability of lawyers for professional conduct, paragraphs (c) and (d) do not create a duty on the lawyer to make any disclosure and no civil liability is intended to arise from the failure to make such disclosure.

15. A lawyer entitled to a fee necessarily must be permitted to prove the services rendered in an action to collect it, and this necessity is

recognized by subparagraphs (c)(5) and (d)(2)(iv). This aspect of the rule, in regard to privileged information, expresses the principle that the beneficiary of a fiduciary relationship may not exploit the relationship to the detriment of the fiduciary. Any disclosure by the lawyer, however, should be as protective of the client's interests as possible.

16. If the client is an organization, a lawyer also should refer to Rule 1.12 in order to determine the appropriate conduct in connection with this Rule.

Client Under a Disability

17. In some situations, Rule 1.02(g) requires a lawyer representing a client under a disability to seek the appointment of a legal representative for the client or to seek other orders for the protection of the client. The client may or may not, in a particular matter, effectively consent to the lawyer's revealing to the court confidential information and facts reasonably necessary to secure the desired appointment or order. Nevertheless, the lawyer is authorized by paragraph (c)(4) to reveal such information in order to comply with Rule 1.02(g). See also paragraph 5, Comment to Rule 1.03.

Mandatory Disclosure Adverse to Client

18. Rule 1.05(e) and (f) place upon a lawyer professional obligations in certain situations to make disclosure in order to prevent certain serious crimes by a client or to prevent involvement by the lawyer in a client's crimes or frauds. Except when death or serious bodily harm is likely to result, a lawyer's initial obligation is to attempt to dissuade the client from committing the crime or fraud or to persuade the client to take corrective action; see Rule 1.02 (d) and (e).

19. Because it is very difficult for a lawyer to know when a client's criminal or fraudulent purpose actually will be carried out, the lawyer is required by paragraph (e) to act only if the lawyer has information "clearly establishing" the likelihood of such acts and consequences. If the information shows clearly that the client's contemplated crime or fraud is likely to result in death or serious injury, the lawyer must seek to avoid those lamentable results by revealing information

necessary to prevent the criminal or fraudulent act. When the threatened crime or fraud is likely to have the less serious result of substantial injury to the financial interests or property of another, the lawyer is not required to reveal preventive information but may do so in conformity to paragraph (c) (7). See also paragraph (f); Rule 1.02 (d) and (e); and Rule 3.03 (b) and (c).

20. Although a violation of paragraph (e) will subject a lawyer to disciplinary action, the lawyer's decisions whether or how to act should not constitute grounds for discipline unless the lawyer's conduct in the light of those decisions was unreasonable under all existing circumstances as they reasonably appeared to the lawyer. This construction necessarily follows from the fact that paragraph (e) bases the lawyer's affirmative duty to act on how the situation "reasonably appears" to the lawyer, while that imposed by paragraph (f) arises only when a lawyer "knows" that the lawyer's services have been misused by the client. See also Rule 3.03(b).

Withdrawal

21. If the lawyer's services will be used by the client in materially furthering a course of criminal or fraudulent conduct, the lawyer must withdraw, as stated in Rule 1.15(a)(1). After withdrawal, a lawyer's conduct continues to be governed by Rule 1.05. The lawyer's duties of mandatory disclosure under paragraph (e) are not affected by termination of the relationship. If disclosure during the relationship was permissive, disclosure thereafter remains permissible under paragraphs (6), (7), and (8) if the further requirements of such paragraph are met. Neither this Rule nor Rule 1. 15 prevents the lawyer from giving notice of the fact of withdrawal, and no rule forbids the lawyer to withdraw or disaffirm any opinion, document, affirmation, or the like.

Other Rules

22. Various other Texas Disciplinary Rules of Professional Conduct permit or require a lawyer to disclose information relating to the representation. See Rules 1.07, 1.12, 2.02, 3.03 and 4.01. In addition to these provisions, a lawyer may be obligated by other provisions of statutes or other law to give information about a client. Whether

another provision of law supersedes Rule 1.05 is a matter of interpretation beyond the scope of these Rules, but subparagraph (c) (4) protects the lawyer from discipline who acts on reasonable belief as to the effect of such laws.

Rule 1.06 Conflict of Interest: General Rule

(a) A lawyer shall not represent opposing parties to the same litigation.

(b) In other situations and except to the extent permitted by paragraph (c), a lawyer shall not represent a person if the representation of that person:

(1) involves a substantially related matter in which that person's interests are materially and directly adverse to the interests of another client of the lawyer or the lawyer's firm; or

(2) reasonably appears to be or become adversely limited by the lawyer's or law firm's responsibilities to another client or to a third person or by the lawyer's or law firm's own interests.

(c) A lawyer may represent a client in the circumstances described in (b) if:

(1) the lawyer reasonably believes the representation of each client will not be materially affected; and

(2) each affected or potentially affected client consents to such representation after full disclosure of the existence, nature, implications, and possible adverse consequences of the common representation and the advantages involved, if any.

(d) A lawyer who has represented multiple parties in a matter shall not thereafter represent any of such parties in a dispute among the parties arising out of the matter, unless prior consent is obtained from all such parties to the dispute.

(e) If a lawyer has accepted representation in violation of this Rule, or if multiple representation properly accepted becomes improper under this Rule, the lawyer shall promptly withdraw from one or more representations to the extent necessary for any remaining representation not to be in violation of these Rules.

(f) If a lawyer would be prohibited by this Rule from engaging in particular conduct, no other lawyer while a member or associated with that lawyer's firm may engage in that conduct.

Comment:

Loyalty to a Client

1. Loyalty is an essential element in the lawyer's relationship to a client. An impermissible conflict of interest may exist before representation is undertaken, in which event the representation should be declined. If such a conflict arises after representation has been undertaken, the lawyer must take effective action to eliminate the conflict, including withdrawal if necessary to rectify the situation. See also Rule 1.16. When more than one client is involved and the lawyer withdraws because a conflict arises after representation, whether the lawyer may continue to represent any of the clients is determined by this Rule and Rules 1.05 and 1.09. See also Rule 1.07(c). Under this Rule, any conflict that prevents a particular lawyer from undertaking or continuing a representation of a client also prevents any other lawyer who is or becomes a member of or an associate with that lawyer's firm from doing so. See paragraph (f).

2. A fundamental principle recognized by paragraph (a) is that a lawyer may not represent opposing parties in litigation. The term "opposing parties" as used in this Rule contemplates a situation where a judgment favorable to one of the parties will directly impact unfavorably upon the other party. Moreover, as a general proposition loyalty to a client prohibits undertaking representation directly adverse to the representation of that client in a substantially related matter unless that client's fully informed consent is obtained and unless the lawyer reasonably believes that the lawyer's representation will be reasonably protective of that client's interests. Paragraphs (b) and (c) express that general concept.

188

Conflicts in Litigation

3. Paragraph (a) prohibits representation of opposing parties in litigation. Simultaneous representation of parties whose interests in litigation are not actually directly adverse but where the potential for conflict exists, such as co-plaintiffs or co-defendants, is governed by paragraph (b). An impermissible conflict may exist or develop by reason of substantial discrepancy in the parties' testimony, incompatibility in positions in relation to an opposing party or the fact that there are substantially different possibilities of settlement of the claims or liabilities in question. Such conflicts can arise in criminal cases as well as civil. The potential for conflict of interest in representing multiple defendants in a criminal case is so grave that ordinarily a lawyer should decline to represent more than one co-defendant. On the other hand, common representation of persons having similar interests is proper if the risk of adverse effect is minimal and the requirements of paragraph (b) are met. Compare Rule 1.07 involving intermediation between clients.

Conflict with Lawyers Own Interests

4. Loyalty to a client is impaired not only by the representation of opposing parties in situations within paragraphs (a) and (b)(1) but also in any situation when a lawyer may not be able to consider, recommend or carry out an appropriate course of action for one client because of the lawyer's own interests or responsibilities to others. The conflict in effect forecloses alternatives that would otherwise be available to the client. Paragraph (b)(2) addresses such situations. A potential possible conflict does not itself necessarily preclude the representation. The critical questions are the likelihood that a conflict exists or will eventuate and, if it does, whether it will materially and adversely affect the lawyer's independent professional judgment in considering alternatives or foreclose courses of action that reasonably should be pursued on behalf of the client. It is for the client to decide whether the client wishes to accommodate the other interest involved. However, the client's consent to the representation by the lawyer of another whose interests are directly adverse is insufficient unless the lawyer also believes that there will be no materially adverse effect upon the interests of either client. See paragraph (c).

5. The lawyer's own interests should not be permitted to have adverse effect on representation of a client, even where paragraph (b)(2 is not

violated. For example, a lawyer's need for income should not lead the lawyer to undertake matters that cannot be handled competently and at a reasonable fee. See Rules 1.01 and 1.04. If the probity of a lawyer's own conduct in a transaction is in question, it may be difficult for the lawyer to give a client detached advice. A lawyer should not allow related business interests to affect representation, for example, by referring clients to an enterprise in which the lawyer has an undisclosed interest.

Meaning of Directly Adverse

6. Within the meaning of Rule 1.06(b), the representation of one client is "directly adverse" to the representation of another client if the lawyer's independent judgment on behalf of a client or the lawyer's ability or willingness to consider, recommend or carry out a course of action will be or is reasonably likely to be adversely affected by the lawyer's representation of, or responsibilities to, the other client. The dual representation also is directly adverse if the lawyer reasonably appears to be called upon to espouse adverse positions in the same matter or a related matter. On the other hand, simultaneous representation in unrelated matters of clients whose interests are only generally adverse, such as competing economic enterprises, does not constitute the representation of directly adverse interests. Even when neither paragraph (a) nor (b) is applicable, a lawyer should realize that a business rivalry or personal differences between two clients or potential clients may be so important to one or both that one or the other would consider it contrary to its interests to have the same lawyer as its rival even in unrelated matters; and in those situations a wise lawyer would forego the dual representation.

Full Disclosure and Informed Consent

7. A client under some circumstances may consent to representation notwithstanding a conflict or potential conflict. However, as indicated in paragraph (c)(1), when a disinterested lawyer would conclude that the client should not agree to the representation under the circumstances, the lawyer involved should not ask for such agreement or provide representation on the basis of the client's consent. When more than one client is involved, the question of conflict must be resolved as to each client. Moreover, there may be circumstances where it is impossible to make the full disclosure necessary to obtain informed consent. For example, when the lawyer represents different clients in related matters

190

and one of the clients refuses to consent to the disclosure necessary to permit the other client to make an informed decision, the lawyer cannot properly ask the latter to consent.

8. Disclosure and consent are not formalities. Disclosure sufficient for sophisticated clients may not be sufficient to permit less sophisticated clients to provide fully informed consent. While it is not required that the disclosure and consent be in writing, it would be prudent for the lawyer to provide potential dual clients with at least a written summary of the considerations disclosed.

9. In certain situations, such as in the preparation of loan papers or the preparation of a partnership agreement, a lawyer might have properly undertaken multiple representation and be confronted subsequently by a dispute among those clients in regard to that matter. Paragraph (d) forbids the representation of any of those parties in regard to that dispute unless informed consent is obtained from all of the parties to the dispute who had been represented by the lawyer in that matter.

10. A lawyer may represent parties having antagonistic positions on a legal question that has arisen in different cases, unless representation of either client would be adversely affected. Thus, it is ordinarily not improper to assert such positions in cases pending in different trial courts, but it may be improper to do so in cases pending at the same time in an appellate court.

11. Ordinarily, it is not advisable for a lawyer to act as advocate against a client the lawyer represents in some other matter, even if the other matter is wholly unrelated and even if paragraphs (a), (b) and (d) are not applicable. However, there are circumstances in which a lawyer may act as advocate against a client, for a lawyer is free to do so unless this Rule or another rule of the Texas Disciplinary Rules of Professional Conduct would be violated. For example, a lawyer representing an enterprise with diverse operations may accept employment as an advocate against the enterprise in a matter unrelated to any matter being handled for the enterprise if the representation of one client is not directly adverse to the representation of the other client. The propriety of concurrent representation can depend on the nature of the litigation. For example, a suit charging fraud entails conflict to a degree not involved in a suit for declaratory judgment concerning statutory interpretation.

Interest of Person Paying for a Lawyer's Service

12. A lawyer may be paid from a source other than the client, if the client is informed of that fact and consents and the arrangement does not compromise the lawyer's duty of loyalty to the client. See Rule 1.08(e). For example, when an insurer and its insured have conflicting interests in a matter arising from a liability insurance agreement, and the insurer is required to provide special counsel for the insured, the arrangement should assure the special counsel's professional independence. So also, when a corporation and its directors or employees are involved in a controversy in which they have conflicting interests, the corporation may provide funds for separate legal representation of the directors or employees, if the clients consent after consultation and the arrangement ensures the lawyer's professional independence.

Non-litigation Conflict Situations

13. Conflicts of interest in contexts other than litigation sometimes may be difficult to assess. Relevant factors in determining whether there is potential for adverse effect include the duration and intimacy of the lawyer's relationship with the client or clients involved, the functions being performed by the lawyer, the likelihood that actual conflict will arise and the likely prejudice to the client from the conflict if it does arise. The question is often one of proximity and degree.

14. For example, a lawyer may not represent multiple parties to a negotiation whose interests are fundamentally antagonistic to each other, but common representation may be permissible where the clients are generally aligned in interest even though there is some difference of interest among them.

15. Conflict questions may also arise in estate planning and estate administration. A lawyer may be called upon to prepare wills for several family members, such as husband and wife, and, depending upon the circumstances, a conflict of interest may arise. In estate administration it may be unclear whether the client is the fiduciary or is the estate or trust, including its beneficiaries. The lawyer should make clear the relationship to the parties involved.

16. A lawyer for a corporation or other organization who is also a member of its board of directors should determine whether the responsibilities of the two roles may conflict. The lawyer may be called on to advise the corporation in matters involving actions of the directors. Consideration should be given to the frequency with which such situations may arise, the potential intensity of the conflict, the effect of the lawyer's resignation from the board and the possibility of the corporation's obtaining legal advice from another lawyer in such situations. If there is material risk that the dual role will compromise the lawyer's independence of professional judgment, the lawyer should not serve as a director.

Conflict Charged by an Opposing Party

17. Raising questions of conflict of interest is primarily the responsibility of the lawyer undertaking the representation. In litigation, a court may raise the question when there is reason to infer that the lawyer has neglected the responsibility. In a criminal case, inquiry by the court is generally required when a lawyer represents multiple defendants. Where the conflict is such as clearly to call in question the fair or efficient administration of justice, opposing counsel may properly raise the question. Such an objection should be viewed with great caution, however, for it can be misused as a technique of harassment. See Preamble: Scope.

18. Except when the absolute prohibition of this rule applies or in litigation when a court passes upon issues of conflicting interests in determining a question of disqualification of counsel, resolving questions of conflict of interests may require decisions by all affected clients as well as by the lawyer.

Rule 1.07 Conflict of Interest: Intermediary

(a) A lawyer shall not act as intermediary between clients unless:

(1) the lawyer consults with each client concerning the implications of the common representation, including the advantages and risks involved, and the effect on the attorney-client privileges, and obtains each client's written consent to the common representation;

(2) the lawyer reasonably believes that the matter can be resolved without the necessity of contested litigation on terms compatible with the clients' best interests, that each client will be able to make adequately informed decisions in the matter and that there is little risk of material prejudice to the interests of any of the clients if the contemplated resolution is unsuccessful; and

(3) the lawyer reasonably believes that the common representation can be undertaken impartially and without improper effect on other responsibilities the lawyer has to any of the clients.

(b) While acting as intermediary, the lawyer shall consult with each client concerning the decision to be made and the considerations relevant in making them, so that each client can make adequately informed decisions.

(c) A lawyer shall withdraw as intermediary if any of the clients so requests, or if any of the conditions stated in paragraph (a) is no longer satisfied. Upon withdrawal, the lawyer shall not continue to represent any of the clients in the matter that was the subject of the intermediation.

(d) Within the meaning of this Rule, a lawyer acts as intermediary if the lawyer represents two or more parties with potentially conflicting interests.

(e) If a lawyer would be prohibited by this Rule from engaging in particular conduct, no other lawyer while a member of or associated with that lawyer's firm may engage in that conduct.

Comment:

1. A lawyer acting as intermediary may seek to establish or adjust a relationship between clients on an amicable and mutually advantageous basis. For example, the lawyer may assist in organizing a business

in which two or more clients are entrepreneurs, in working out the financial reorganization of an enterprise in which two or more clients have an interest, in arranging a property distribution in settlement of an estate or in mediating a dispute between clients. The lawyer seeks to resolve potentially conflicting interests by developing the parties' mutual interests. The alternative can be that each party may have to obtain separate representation, with the possibility in some situations of incurring additional cost, complication or even litigation. Given these and other relevant factors, all the clients may prefer that the lawyer act as intermediary.

2. Because confusion can arise as to the lawyer's role where each party is not separately represented, it is important that the lawyer make clear the relationship; hence, the requirement of written consent. Moreover, a lawyer should not permit his personal interests to influence his advice relative to a suggestion by his client that additional counsel be employed. See also Rule 1.06 (b).

3. The Rule does not apply to a lawyer acting as arbitrator or mediator between or among parties who are not clients of the lawyer, even where the lawyer has been appointed with the concurrence of the parties. In performing such a role the lawyer may be subject to applicable codes of ethics, such as the Code of Ethics for Arbitration in Commercial Disputes prepared by a joint Committee of the American Bar Association and the American Arbitration Association.

4. In considering whether to act as intermediary between clients, a lawyer should be mindful that if the intermediation fails the result can be additional cost, embarrassment and recrimination. In some situations, the risk of failure is so great that intermediation is plainly impossible. Moreover, a lawyer cannot undertake common representation of clients between whom contested litigation is reasonably expected or who contemplate contentious negotiations. More generally, if the relationship between the parties has already assumed definite antagonism, the possibility that the clients' interests can be adjusted by intermediation ordinarily is not very good.

5. The appropriateness of intermediation can depend on its form. Forms of intermediation range from informal arbitration, where each client's case is presented by the respective client and the lawyer decides the

outcome, to mediation, to common representation where the clients' interests are substantially though not entirely compatible. One form may be appropriate in circumstances where another would not. Other relevant factors are whether the lawyer subsequently will represent both parties on a continuing basis and whether the situation involves creating a relationship between the parties or terminating one.

Confidentiality and Privilege

6. A particular important factor in determining the appropriateness of intermediation is the effect on client-lawyer confidentiality and the attorney-client privilege. In a common representation, the lawyer is still required both to keep each client adequately informed and to maintain confidentiality of information relating to the representation, except as to such clients. See Rules 1.03 and 1.05. Complying with both requirements while acting as intermediary requires a delicate balance. If the balance cannot be maintained, the common representation is improper. With regard to the attorney-client privilege, the general rule is that as between commonly represented clients the privilege does not attach. Hence, it must be assumed that if litigation eventuates between the clients, the privilege will not protect any such communications, and the clients should be so advised.

7. Since the lawyer is required to be impartial between commonly represented clients, intermediation is improper when that impartiality cannot be maintained. For example, a lawyer who has represented one of the clients for a long period and in a variety of matters might have difficulty being impartial between that client and one to whom the lawyer has only recently been introduced.

Consultation

8. In acting as intermediary between clients, the lawyer should consult with the clients on the implications of doing so, and proceed only upon informed consent based on such a consultation. The consultation should make clear that the lawyer's role is not that of partisanship normally expected in other circumstances.

9. Paragraph (b) is an application of the principle expressed in Rule 1.03. Where the lawyer is intermediary, the clients ordinarily must assume

196

greater responsibility for decisions than when each client is independently represented.

10. Under this Rule, any condition or circumstance that prevents a particular lawyer either from acting as intermediary between clients, or from representing those clients individually in connection with a matter after an unsuccessful intermediation, also prevents any other lawyer who is or becomes a member of or associates with that lawyer's firm from doing so. See paragraphs (c) and (e).

Withdrawal

11. In the event of withdrawal by one or more parties from the enterprise, the lawyer may continue to act for the remaining parties and the enterprise. See also Rule 1.06 (c) (2) which authorizes continuation of the representation with consent.

Rule 1.08 Conflict of Interest: Prohibited Transactions

(a) A lawyer shall not enter into a business transaction with a client unless:

(1) the transaction and terms on which the lawyer acquires the interest are fair and reasonable to the client and are fully disclosed in a manner which can be reasonably understood by the client;

(2) the client is given a reasonable opportunity to seek the advice of independent counsel in the transaction; and

 (3) the client consents in writing thereto.

(b) A lawyer shall not prepare an instrument giving the lawyer or a person related to the lawyer as a parent, child, sibling, or spouse any substantial gift from a client, including a testamentary gift, except where the client is related to the donee.

(c) Prior to the conclusion of all aspects of the matter giving rise to the lawyer's employment, a lawyer shall not make or negotiate an agreement with a client, prospective client, or former client giving the lawyer literary or media rights to a portrayal or account based in substantial part on information relating to the representation.

(d) A lawyer shall not provide financial assistance to a client in connection with pending or contemplated litigation or administrative proceedings, except that:

(1) a lawyer may advance or guarantee court costs, expenses of litigation or administrative proceedings, and reasonably necessary medical and living expenses, the repayment of which may be contingent on the outcome of the matter; and

(2) a lawyer representing an indigent client may pay court costs and expenses of litigation on behalf of the client.

(e) A lawyer shall not accept compensation for representing a client from one other than the client unless:

(1) the client consents;

(2) there is no interference with the lawyer's independence of professional judgment or with the client-lawyer relationship; and

(3) information relating to representation of a client is protected as required by Rule 1.05.

(f) A lawyer who represents two or more clients shall not participate in making an aggregate settlement of the claims of or against the clients, or in a criminal case an aggregated agreement to guilty or nolo contendere pleas, unless each client has consented after consultation, including disclosure of the existence and nature of all the claims or pleas involved and of the nature and extent of the participation of each person in the settlement.

(g) A lawyer shall not make an agreement prospectively limiting the lawyer's liability to a client for malpractice unless permitted by law and the client is independently represented in making the agreement, or settle a claim for such liability with an unrepresented client or former client without first advising that person in writing that independent representation is appropriate in connection therewith.

(h) A lawyer shall not acquire a proprietary interest in the cause of action or subject matter of litigation the lawyer is conducting for a client, except that the lawyer may:

(1) acquire a lien granted by law to secure the lawyer's fee or expenses; and

(2) contract in a civil case with a client for a contingent fee that is permissible under Rule 1.04.

(i) If a lawyer would be prohibited by this Rule from engaging in particular conduct, no other lawyer while a member of or associated with that lawyer's firm may engage in that conduct.

(j) As used in this Rule, "business transactions" does not include standard commercial transactions between the lawyer and the client for products or services that the client generally markets to others.

Comment:

Transactions between Client and Lawyer

1. This rule deals with certain transactions that per se involve unacceptable conflicts of interests.

2. As a general principle, all transactions between client and lawyer should be fair and reasonable to the client. In such transactions, a review by independent counsel on behalf of the client is often advisable. Paragraph (a) does not, however, apply to standard commercial transactions between the lawyer and the client for products or services that the client generally markets to others, such as banking or brokerage services, medical services, products manufactured or distributed by the client, and utilities services. In such transactions, the lawyer has no advantage in dealing with the client, and the restrictions in paragraph (a) are unnecessary and impracticable.

3. A lawyer may accept a gift from a client, if the transaction meets general standards of fairness. For example, a simple gift such as a present given at a holiday or as a token of appreciation is permitted. If effectuation of a substantial gift requires preparing a legal instrument such as a will or conveyance, however, the client should have the detached advice that another lawyer can provide. Paragraph (b) recognizes an exception where the client is a relative of the donee or the gift is not substantial.

Literary Rights

4. An agreement by which a lawyer acquires literary or media rights concerning the conduct of representation creates a conflict between the interests of the client and the personal interests of the lawyer. Measures suitable in the representation of the client may detract from the publication value of an account of the representation. Paragraph (c) does not prohibit a lawyer representing a client in a transaction concerning literary property from agreeing that the lawyer's fee shall consist of a share in ownership in the property, if the arrangement conforms to Rule 1.04 and to paragraph (h) of this Rule.

Person Paying for Lawyer's Services

5. Paragraph (e) requires disclosure to the client of the fact that the lawyer's services are being paid for by a third party. Such an arrangement must also conform to the requirements of Rule 1.05 concerning confidentiality and Rule 1.06 concerning conflict of interest. Where the client is a class, consent may be obtained on behalf of the class by court-supervised procedure. Where an insurance company pays the lawyer's fee for representing an insured, normally the insured has consented to the arrangement by the terms of the insurance contract.

Prospectively Limiting Liability

6. Paragraph (g) is not intended to apply to customary qualification and limitations in legal opinions and memoranda.

Acquisition of Interest in Litigation

7. This Rule embodies the traditional general precept that lawyers are prohibited from acquiring a proprietary interest in the subject matter

of litigation. This general precept, which has its basis in common law champerty and maintenance, is subject to specific exceptions developed in decisional law and continued in these Rules, such as the exception for contingent fees set forth in Rule 1.04 and the exception for certain advances of the costs of litigation set forth in paragraph (d). A special instance arises when a lawyer proposes to incur litigation or other expenses with an entity in which the lawyer has a pecuniary interest. A lawyer should not incur such expenses unless the client has entered into a written agreement complying with paragraph (a) that contains a full disclosure of the nature and amount of the possible expenses and the relationship between the lawyer and the other entity involved.

Imputed Disqualifications

8. The prohibitions imposed on an individual lawyer by this Rule are imposed by paragraph (i) upon all other lawyers while practicing with that lawyer's firm.

Rule 1.09 Conflict of Interest: Former Client

(a) Without prior consent, a lawyer who personally has formerly represented a client in a matter shall not thereafter represent another person in a matter adverse to the former client:

(1) in which such other person questions the validity of the lawyer's services or work product for the former client;

(2) if the representation in reasonable probability will involve a violation of Rule 1.05; or

(3) if it is the same or a substantially related matter.

(b) Except to the extent authorized by Rule 1.10, when lawyers are or have become members of or associated with a firm, none of them shall knowingly represent a client if any one of them practicing alone would be prohibited from doing so by paragraph (a).

(c)When the association of a lawyer with a firm has terminated, the lawyers who were then associated with that lawyer shall not knowingly represent a client if the lawyer whose association with that firm has terminated would be prohibited from doing so by paragraph (a)(1) or if the representation in reasonable probability will involve a violation of Rule 1.05.

Comment:

1. Rule 1.09 addresses the circumstances in which a lawyer in private practice, and other lawyers who were, are or become members of or associated with a firm in which that lawyer practiced or practices, may represent a client against a former client of that lawyer or the lawyer's former firm. Whether a lawyer, or that lawyer's present or former firm, is prohibited from representing a client in a matter by reason of the lawyer's successive government and private employment is governed by Rule 1.10 rather than by this Rule.

2. Paragraph (a) concerns the situation where a lawyer once personally represented a client and now wishes to represent a second client against that former client. Whether such a personal attorney-client relationship existed involves questions of both fact and law that are beyond the scope of these Rules. See Preamble: Scope. Among the relevant factors, however, would be how the former representation actually was conducted within the firm; the nature and scope of the former client's contacts with the firm (including any restrictions the client may have placed on the dissemination of confidential information within the firm); and the size of the firm.

3. Although paragraph (a) does not absolutely prohibit a lawyer from representing a client against a former client, it does provide that the latter representation is improper if any of three circumstances exists, except with prior consent. The first circumstance is that the lawyer may not represent a client who questions the validity of the lawyer's services or work product for the former client. Thus, for example, a lawyer who drew a will leaving a substantial portion of the testator's property to a designated beneficiary would violate paragraph (a) by representing the testator's heirs at law in an action seeking to overturn the will.

4. Paragraph (a)'s second limitation on undertaking a representation against a former client is that it may not be done if there is a "reasonable probability" that the representation would cause the lawyer to violate the obligations owed the former client under Rule 1.05. Thus, for example, if there were a reasonable probability that the subsequent representation would involve either an unauthorized disclosure of confidential information under Rule 1.05 (b) (1) or an improper use of such information to the disadvantage of the former client under Rule 1.05 (b) (3), that representation would be improper under paragraph (a). Whether such a reasonable probability exists in any given case will be a question of fact.

4A. The third situation where representation adverse to a former client is prohibited is where the representation involves the same or a substantially related matter. The "same" matter aspect of this prohibition prevents a lawyer from switching sides and representing a party whose interests are adverse to a person who disclosed confidences to the lawyer while seeking in good faith to retain the lawyer. The prohibition applies when an actual attorney-client was established even if the lawyer withdrew from the representation before the client had disclosed any confidential information. This aspect of the prohibition includes, but is somewhat broader than, that contained in paragraph (a) (1) of this Rule.

4B. The "substantially related" aspect, on the other hand, has a different focus. Although that term is not defined in the Rule, it primarily involves situations where a lawyer could have acquired confidential information concerning a prior client that could be used either to that prior client's disadvantage or for the advantage of the lawyer's current client or some other person. It thus largely overlaps the prohibition contained in paragraph (a) (2) of this Rule.

5. Paragraph (b) extends paragraph (a)'s limitations on an individual lawyer's freedom to undertake a representation against that lawyer's former client to all other lawyers who are or become members of or associated with the firm in which that lawyer is practicing. Thus, for example, if a client severs the attorney-client relationship with a lawyer who remains in a firm, the entitlement of that individual lawyer to undertake a representation against that former client is governed by paragraph (a); and all other lawyers who are or become members of or associated with that lawyer's firm are treated in the same manner by paragraph (b). Similarly, if a lawyer severs his or her association with a firm and that firm retains as

a client a person whom the lawyer personally represented while with the firm, that lawyer's ability thereafter to undertake a representation against that client is governed by paragraph (a); and all other lawyers who are or become members of or associates with that lawyer's new firm are treated in the same manner by paragraph (b).

6. Paragraph (c) addresses the situation of former partners or associates of a lawyer who once had represented a client when the relationship between the former partners or associates and the lawyer has been terminated. In that situation, the former partners or associates are prohibited from questioning the validity of such lawyer's work product and from undertaking representation which in reasonable probability will involve a violation of Rule 1.05. Such a violation could occur, for example, when the former partners or associates retained materials in their files from the earlier representation of the client that, if disclosed or used in connection with the subsequent representation, would violate Rule 1.05(b)(1) or (b)(3).

7. Thus, the effect of paragraph (b) is to extend any inability of a particular lawyer under paragraph (a) to undertake a representation against a former client to all other lawyers who are or become members of or associated with any firm in which that lawyer is practicing. If, on the other hand, a lawyer disqualified by paragraph (a) should leave a firm, paragraph (c) prohibits lawyers remaining in that firm from undertaking a representation that would be forbidden to the departed lawyer only if that representation would violate subparagraphs (a)(1) or (a)(2). Finally, should those other lawyers cease to be members of the same firm as the lawyer affected by paragraph (a) without personally coming within its restrictions, they thereafter may undertake the representation against the lawyer's former client unless prevented from doing so by some other of these Rules.

8. Although not required to do so by Rule 1.05 or this Rule, some courts, as a procedural decision, disqualify a lawyer for representing a present client against a former client when the subject matter of the present representation is so closely related to the subject matter of the prior representation that confidences obtained from the former client might be useful in the representation of the present client. See Comment 17 to Rule 1.06. This so-called "substantial relationship" test is defended by asserting that to require a showing that confidences of the first client were in fact used for the benefit of the subsequent client as a condition to procedural

disqualification would cause disclosure of the confidences that the court seeks to protect. A lawyer is not subject to discipline under Rule 1.05(b) (1), (3), or (4), however, unless the protected information is actually used. Likewise, a lawyer is not subject to discipline under this Rule unless the new representation by the lawyer in reasonable probability would result in a violation of those provisions.

9. Whether the "substantial relationship" test will continue to be employed as a standard for procedural disqualification is a matter beyond the scope of these Rules. See Preamble: Scope. The possibility that such a disqualification might be sought by the former client or granted by a court, however, is a matter that could be of substantial importance to the present client in deciding whether or not to retain or continue to employ a particular lawyer or law firm as its counsel. Consequently, a lawyer should disclose those possibilities, as well as their potential consequences for the representation, to the present client as soon as the lawyer becomes aware of them; and the client then should be allowed to decide whether or not to obtain new counsel. See Rules 1.03(b) and 1.06(b).

10. This Rule is primarily for the protection of clients and its protections can be waived by them. A waiver is effective only if there is consent after disclosure of the relevant circumstances, including the lawyer's past or intended role on behalf of each client, as appropriate. See Comments 7 and 8 to Rule 1.06.

Rule 1.11 Adjudicatory Official or Law Clerk

(a)A lawyer shall not represent anyone in connection with a matter in which the lawyer has passed upon the merits or otherwise participated personally and substantially as an adjudicatory official or law clerk to an adjudicatory official, unless all parties to the proceeding consent after disclosure.

(b)   A lawyer who is an adjudicatory official shall not negotiate for employment with any person who is involved as a party or as attorney for a party in a pending matter in which that official is participating personally and substantially. A lawyer serving as a law clerk to an adjudicatory official may negotiate for employment with a party or attorney involved in a matter in which the clerk is participating personally and substantially, but only after the clerk has notified the adjudicatory official.

(c)If paragraph (a) is applicable to a lawyer, no other lawyer in a firm with which that lawyer is associated may knowingly undertake or continue representation in the matter unless:

(1) the lawyer who is subject to paragraph (a) is screened from participation in the matter and is apportioned no part of the fee therefrom; and

(2) written notice is promptly given to the other parties to the proceeding.

Comment:

1. This Rule generally parallels Rule 1.10. The term "personally and substantially" signifies that a judge who was a member of a multi-member court and thereafter left judicial office to practice law is not prohibited from representing a client in a matter pending in the court but in which the former judge did not participate. So also the fact that a former judge exercised administrative responsibility in a court does not prevent the former judge from acting as a lawyer in matters where the judge had previously exercised remote or incidental administrative responsibility that did not affect the merits. Compare the Comments to Rule 1.10.

2. The term "Adjudicatory Official" includes not only judges but also comparable officials serving on tribunals, such as judges pro tempore, referees, special masters, hearing officers and other parajudicial officers, as well as lawyers who serve as part-time judges. Compliance provisions B(2) and C of the Texas Code of Judicial Conduct provide that a part-time judge or judge pro tempore may not "act as a lawyer in a proceeding in which he has served as a judge or in any other proceeding related thereto." Although phrased differently from this rule, those provisions correspond in meaning.

3. Some law clerks have not been licensed as lawyers at the time they commence service as law clerks. Obviously, paragraph (b) cannot apply

to a law clerk until the clerk has been licensed as a lawyer. Paragraph (a) applies, however, to a lawyer without regard to whether the lawyer had been licensed at the time of the service as a law clerk, and once that law clerk is licensed as a lawyer and joins a firm, paragraph (c) applies to the firm.

4. Paragraph (c) does not prohibit a lawyer from receiving a salary or partnership share established by prior independent agreement. It prohibits directly relating the lawyer's compensation to the fee in the matter in which the lawyer is disqualified.

Rule 1.15 Declining or Terminating Representation

(a)A lawyer shall decline to represent a client or, where representation has commenced, shall withdraw, except as stated in paragraph (c), from the representation of a client, if:

(1) the representation will result in violation of Rule 3.08, other applicable rules of professional conduct or other law;

(2) the lawyer's physical, mental or psychological condition materially impairs the lawyer's fitness to represent the client; or

(3) the lawyer is discharged, with or without good cause.

(b) Except as required by paragraph (a), a lawyer shall not withdraw from representing a client unless:

(1) withdrawal can be accomplished without material adverse effect on the interests of the client;

(2) the client persists in a course of action involving the lawyer's services that the lawyer reasonably believes may be criminal or fraudulent;

(3) the client has used the lawyer's services to perpetrate a crime or fraud;

(4) a client insists upon pursuing an objective that the lawyer considers repugnant or imprudent or with which the lawyer has fundamental disagreement;

(5) the client fails substantially to fulfill an obligation to the lawyer regarding the lawyer's services, including an obligation to pay the lawyer's fee as agreed, and has been given reasonable warning that the lawyer will withdraw unless the obligation is fulfilled;

(6) the representation will result in an unreasonable financial burden on the lawyer or has been rendered unreasonably difficult by the client; or

(7) other good cause for withdrawal exists.

(c)When ordered to do so by a tribunal, a lawyer shall continue representation notwithstanding good cause for terminating the representation.

(d) Upon termination of representation, a lawyer shall take steps to the extent reasonably practicable to protect a client's interests, such as giving reasonable notice to the client, allowing time for employment of other counsel, surrendering papers and property to which the client is entitled and refunding any advance payments of fee that has not been earned. The lawyer may retain papers relating to the client to the extent permitted by other law only if such retention will not prejudice the client in the subject matter of the representation.

Comment:

1. A lawyer should not accept representation in a matter unless it can be performed competently, promptly, and without improper conflict of interest. See generally Rules 1.01, 1.06, 1.07, 1.08, and 1.09. Having accepted the representation, a lawyer normally should endeavor to handle the matter to completion. Nevertheless, in certain situations the lawyer must terminate the representation and in certain other situations the lawyer is permitted to withdraw.

Mandatory Withdrawal

2. A lawyer ordinarily must decline employment if the employment will cause the lawyer to engage in conduct that the lawyer knows is illegal or that violates the Texas Disciplinary Rules of Professional Conduct. Rule 1.15(a)(1); cf. Rules 1.02(c), 3.01, 3.02, 3.03, 3.04, 3.08, 4.01, and 8.04. Similarly, paragraph (a)(1) of this Rule requires a lawyer to withdraw from employment when the lawyer knows that the employment will result in a violation of a rule of professional conduct or other law. The lawyer is not obliged to decline or withdraw simply because the client suggests such a course of conduct; a client may have made such a suggestion in the ill-founded hope that a lawyer will not be constrained by a professional obligation. Cf. Rule 1.02(c) and (d).

3. When a lawyer has been appointed to represent a client and in certain other instances in litigation, withdrawal ordinarily requires approval of the appointing authority or presiding judge. See also Rule 6.01. Difficulty may be encountered if withdrawal is based on the client's demand that the lawyer engage in unprofessional conduct. The tribunal may wish an explanation for the withdrawal, while the lawyer may be bound to keep confidential the facts that would constitute such an explanation. The lawyer's statement that professional considerations require termination of the representation ordinarily should be accepted as sufficient. See also Rule 1.06(e).

Discharge

4. A client has the power to discharge a lawyer at any time, with or without cause, subject to liability for payment for the lawyer's services, and paragraph (a) of this Rule requires that the discharged lawyer withdraw. Where future dispute about the withdrawal may be anticipated, it may be advisable to prepare a written statement reciting the circumstances.

5. Whether a client can discharge an appointed counsel depends on the applicable law. A client seeking to do so should be given full explanation of the consequences. In some instances the consequences may include a decision by the appointing authority or presiding judge that appointment of successor counsel is unjustified, thus requiring the client to represent himself.

Mentally Incompetent Client

6. If the client is mentally incompetent, the client may lack the legal capacity to discharge the lawyer (see paragraphs 11 and 12 of Comment to Rule 1.02), and in any event the discharge may be seriously adverse to the client's interests. The lawyer should make special effort to help the incompetent client consider the consequences (see paragraph 5 of Comment to Rule 1.03) and in some situations may initiate proceedings for a conservatorship or similar protection of the client. See Rule 1.02(e).

Optional Withdrawal

7. Paragraph (b) supplements paragraph (a) by permitting a lawyer to withdraw from representation in some certain additional circumstances. The lawyer has the option to withdraw if it can be accomplished without material adverse effect on the client's interests. Withdrawal is also justified if the client persists in a course of action that the lawyer reasonably believes is criminal or fraudulent, for a lawyer is not required to be associated with such conduct even if the lawyer does not further it. A lawyer is not required to discontinue the representation until the lawyer knows the conduct will be illegal or in violation of these rules, at which point the lawyer's withdrawal is mandated by paragraph (a)(1). Withdrawal is also permitted if the lawyer's services were misused in the past. The lawyer also may withdraw where the client insists on pursuing a repugnant or imprudent objective or one with which the lawyer has fundamental disagreement. A lawyer may withdraw if the client refuses, after being duly warned, to abide by the terms of an agreement relating to the representation, such as an agreement concerning fees or court costs or an agreement limiting the objectives of the representation.

8. Withdrawal permitted by paragraph (b)(2) through (7) is optional with the lawyer even though the withdrawal may have a material adverse effect upon the interests of the client.

Assisting the Client Upon Withdrawal

9. In every instance of withdrawal and even if the lawyer has been unfairly discharged by the client, a lawyer must take all reasonable steps to mitigate the consequences to the client. See paragraph (d). The lawyer may retain papers as security for a fee only to the extent permitted by law.

10. Other rules, in addition to Rule 1.15, require or suggest withdrawal in certain situations. See Rules 1.01, 1.05 Comment 22, 1.06(e) and 1.07(c), 1.11(c), 1.12(d), and 3.08(a).

3.08 Lawyer as Witness

(a)A lawyer shall not accept or continue employment as an advocate before a tribunal in a contemplated or pending adjudicatory proceeding if the lawyer knows or believes that the lawyer is or may be a witness necessary to establish an essential fact on behalf of the lawyer's client, unless:

(1) the testimony relates to an uncontested issue;

(2) the testimony will relate solely to a matter of formality and there is no reason to believe that substantial evidence will be offered in opposition to the testimony;

(3) the testimony relates to the nature and value of legal services rendered in the case;

(4) the lawyer is a party to the action and is appearing prose; or

(5) the lawyer has promptly notified opposing counsel that the lawyer expects to testify in the matter and disqualification of the lawyer would work substantial hardship on the client.

(b) A lawyer shall not continue as an advocate in a pending adjudicatory proceeding if the lawyer believes that the lawyer will be compelled to furnish testimony that will be substantially adverse to the lawyer's client, unless the client consents after full disclosure.

(c)Without the client's informed consent, a lawyer may not act as advocate in an adjudicatory proceeding in which another lawyer in the lawyer's firm is prohibited by paragraphs (a) or (b) from serving as advocate. If the lawyer to be called as a witness could not also serve as an advocate under this Rule, that lawyer shall not take an active role before the tribunal in the presentation of the matter.

Comment:

1. A lawyer who is considering accepting or continuing employment in a contemplated or pending adjudicatory proceeding in which that lawyer knows or believes that he or she may be a necessary witness is obligated by this Rule to consider the possible consequences of those dual roles for both the lawyer's own client and for opposing parties.

2. One important variable in this context is the anticipated tenor of the lawyer's testimony. If that testimony will be substantially adverse to the client, paragraphs (b) and (c) provide the governing standard. In other situations, paragraphs (a) and (c) control.

3. A lawyer who is considering both representing a client in an adjudicatory proceeding and serving as a witness in that proceeding may possess information pertinent to the representation that would be substantially adverse to the client were it to be disclosed. A lawyer who believes that he or she will be compelled to furnish testimony concerning such matters should not continue to act as an advocate for his or her client except with the client's informed consent, because of the substantial likelihood that such adverse testimony would damage the lawyer's ability to represent the client effectively.

4. In all other circumstances, the principal concern over allowing a lawyer to serve as both an advocate and witness for a client is the possible confusion that those dual roles could create for the finder of fact. Normally those dual roles are unlikely to create exceptional difficulties when the lawyer's testimony is limited to the areas set out in subparagraphs (a) (1)-(4) of this Rule. If, however, the lawyer's testimony concerns a controversial or contested matter, combining the roles of advocate and witness can unfairly prejudice the opposing party. A witness is required to testify on the basis of personal knowledge, while an advocate is expected to explain and comment on evidence given by others. It may not be clear whether a statement by an advocate-witness should be taken as proof or as an analysis of the proof.

5. Paragraph (a)(1) recognizes that if the testimony will be uncontested, the ambiguities in the dual role are purely theoretical. Paragraph (a)(2) recognizes that similar considerations apply if a lawyer's testimony relates solely to a matter of formality and there is no reason to believe that substantial opposing evidence will be offered. In each of those situations requiring the involvement of another lawyer would be a costly procedure that would serve no significant countervailing purpose.

6. Subparagraph (a)(3) recognizes that where the testimony concerns the extent and value of legal services rendered in the action in which the testimony is offered, permitting the lawyers to testify avoids the need for a second trial with new counsel to resolve that issue. Moreover, in such a situation the judge has firsthand knowledge of the matter in issue; hence, there is less dependence on the adversary process to test the credibility of the testimony. Subparagraph (a)(4) makes it clear that this Rule is not intended to affect a lawyer's right to self-representation.

7. Apart from these four exceptions, subparagraph (a)(5) recognizes an additional exception based upon a balancing of the interests of the client and those of the opposing party. In implementing this exception, it is relevant that one or both parties could reasonably foresee that the lawyer would probably be a witness. For example, subparagraph (a)(5) requires that a lawyer relying on that subparagraph as a basis for serving as both an advocate and a witness for a party give timely notification of that fact to opposing counsel. That requirement serves two purposes. First, it prevents the testifying lawyer from creating a "substantial hardship," where none once existed, by virtue of a lengthy representation of the client in the matter at hand. Second, it puts opposing parties on notice of the situation, thus enabling them to make any desired response at the earliest opportunity.

8. This rule does not prohibit the lawyer who may or will be a witness from participating in the preparation of a matter for presentation to a tribunal. To minimize the possibility of unfair prejudice to an opposing party, however, the Rule prohibits any testifying lawyer who could not serve as an advocate from taking an active role before the tribunal in the presentation of the matter. See paragraph (c). Even in those situations, however, another lawyer in the testifying lawyer's firm may act as an advocate, provided the client's informed consent is obtained.

9. Rule 3.08 sets out a disciplinary standard and is not well suited to use as a standard for procedural disqualification. As a disciplinary rule it serves two principal purposes. The first is to insure that a client's case is not compromised by being represented by a lawyer who could be a more effective witness for the client by not also serving as an advocate. See paragraph (a). The second is to insure that a client is not burdened by counsel who may have to offer testimony that is substantially adverse to the client's cause. See paragraph (b).

10. This Rule may furnish some guidance in those procedural disqualification disputes where the party seeking disqualification can demonstrate actual prejudice to itself resulting from the opposing lawyer's service in the dual roles. However, it should not be used as a tactical weapon to deprive the opposing party of the right to be represented by the lawyer of his or her choice. For example, a lawyer should not seek to disqualify an opposing lawyer under this Rule merely because the opposing lawyer's dual roles may involve an improper conflict of interest with respect to the opposing lawyer's client, for that is a matter to be resolved between lawyer and client or in a subsequent disciplinary proceeding. Likewise, a lawyer should not seek to disqualify an opposing lawyer by unnecessarily calling that lawyer as a witness. Such unintended applications of this Rule, if allowed, would subvert its true purpose by converting it into a mere tactical weapon in litigation.